J. B. Priestley writes:

"*The Last Enemy* differs from all other books about the RAF because its author, Richard Hillary, is by temperament and inclination, and to some extent training, a writer.

"When the war broke out he was still at Oxford. Then he obtained a commission in the RAF and became, after a period of preparation that he describes with admirable skill, a fighter pilot. He fought in the Battle of Britain, but was shot down in flames ... He spent month after month in various hospitals, sometimes making rapid progress towards recovery and then suffering heartbreaking setbacks.

"The value of this book lies in the fact that it is the statement of a fully articulate young man about life in a service which is generally inarticulate ... Richard Hillary happens to be a kind of young man who doesn't often find his way into the RAF. He is in my view a born writer.

"In the opening chapters there is no war and we are reading about how life looked to an Oxford Third Year Man, but even so we are entertained and held simply because Richard Hillary is a real writer. And I hope he goes on writing. Just as once there was a place for him in the air, now there is plenty of room for him on the ground. Welcome, colleague!"

RICHARD HILLARY was killed in action in 1943, nine months after this review was written.

"The last enemy that shall be destroyed is death"—

CORINTHIANS XV, 26

# THE LAST ENEMY

## RICHARD HILLARY

UNABRIDGED

PAN BOOKS LTD : LONDON

First published 1942 by Macmillan & Co., Ltd.
This edition published 1956 by Pan Books Ltd.,
33 Tothill Street, London, S.W.1

330 02406 x

2nd Printing 1957
3rd Printing (New Edition) 1960
4th Printing 1969

Printed in Great Britain

FOR
D. M. W.

# CONTENTS

This book is sold subject to the condition that it shall not, by way of trade, be lent, re-sold, hired out, or otherwise disposed of without the publisher's consent, in any form of binding or cover other than that in which it is published.

# PROEM

SEPTEMBER 3 dawned dark and overcast, with a slight breeze ruffling the waters of the Estuary. Hornchurch aerodrome, twelve miles east of London, wore its usual morning pallor of yellow fog, lending an added air of grimness to the dimly silhouetted Spitfires around the boundary. From time to time a balloon would poke its head grotesquely through the mist as though looking for possible victims before falling back like some tired monster.

We came out on to the tarmac at about eight o'clock. During the night our machines had been moved from the Dispersal Point over to the hangars. All the machine tools, oil, and general equipment had been left on the far side of the aerodrome. I was worried. We had been bombed a short time before, and my plane had been fitted out with a new cockpit hood. This hood unfortunately would not slide open along its groove ; and with a depleted ground staff and no tools, I began to fear it never would. Unless it did open, I shouldn't be able to bale out in a hurry if I had to. Miraculously, " Uncle George " Denholm,

1

our Squadron Leader, produced three men with a heavy file and lubricating oil, and the corporal fitter and I set upon the hood in a fury of haste. We took it turn by turn, filing and oiling, oiling and filing, until at last the hood began to move. But agonizingly slowly : by ten o'clock, when the mist had cleared and the sun was blazing out of a clear sky, the hood was still sticking firmly half-way along the groove ; at ten-fifteen, what I had feared for the last hour happened. Down the loud-speaker came the emotion-less voice of the controller : " 603 Squadron take off and patrol base ; you will receive further orders in the air : 603 Squadron take off as quickly as you can, please." As I pressed the starter and the engine roared into life, the corporal stepped back and crossed his fingers significantly. I felt the usual sick feeling in the pit of the stomach, as though I were about to row a race, and then I was too busy getting into position to feel anything.

Uncle George and the leading section took off in a cloud of dust ; Brian Carbury looked across and put up his thumbs. I nodded and opened up, to take off for the last time from Hornchurch. I was flying No. 3 in Brian's section, with Stapme Stapleton on the right : the third section consisted of only two machines, so that our Squadron strength was eight. We headed south-east, climbing all out on a steady course. At about 12,000 feet we came up through the clouds : I looked down and saw them spread out below me like layers of whipped cream. The sun was brilliant and made it difficult to see even the next plane when turning. I was peering anxiously ahead, for the controller had given us warning of at least fifty enemy fighters approaching very high. When we did first sight them, nobody shouted, as I think we all saw them at the same moment. They must have been 500 to 1000 feet above us and coming straight on like a swarm of locusts. I remember cursing and going automatically into line astern : the next moment we were in among them and it was each man for himself. As soon as they saw us they spread out and dived, and the next ten minutes was a blur of twisting machines and tracer bullets. One Messerschmitt went down in a sheet of flame on my right, and a Spitfire hurtled past in a half-roll ; I was weaving and turning in a desperate attempt to gain height, with the machine practically hanging on the airscrew. Then, just below me and to my left, I saw what I had been praying for — a Messerschmitt climbing and away from the sun. I closed in to 200 yards, and from slightly to one side gave him a two-second burst : fabric ripped off the wing and black smoke poured from the engine, but he did not go down. Like a fool, I did not break away, but put in another three-second burst. Red flames shot upwards and he spiralled out of sight. At that moment, I felt a terrific explosion which knocked the control stick from my hand, and the whole machine quivered like a stricken animal. In a second, the cockpit was a mass of flames : instinctively, I reached up to open the hood. It would not move. I tore off my straps and managed to force it back ; but this took time, and when I dropped back into the seat and reached for the stick in an effort to turn the plane on its back, the heat was so intense that I could feel myself going. I remember a second of sharp agony, remember thinking " So this is it ! " and putting both hands to my eyes. Then I passed out.

When I regained consciousness I was free of the machine and falling rapidly. I pulled the rip-cord of my parachute and checked my descent with a jerk. Looking down, I saw that my left trouser leg was burnt off, that I was going to fall into the sea, and that the English coast was deplorably far away. About twenty feet above the water, I attempted to undo my parachute, failed, and flopped into the sea with it billowing round me. I was told later that the machine went into a spin at about 25,000 feet and that at 10,000 feet I fell out — unconscious. This may well have been so, for I discovered later a large cut on the top of my head, presumably collected while bumping round inside.

The water was not unwarm and I was pleasantly surprised to find that my life-jacket kept me afloat.

4

I looked at my watch : it was not there. Then, for the first time, I noticed how burnt my hands were : down to the wrist, the skin was dead white and hung in shreds : I felt faintly sick from the smell of burnt flesh. By closing one eye I could see my lips, jutting out like motor tyres. The side of my parachute harness was cutting into me particularly painfully, so that I guessed my right hip was burnt. I made a further attempt to undo the harness, but owing to the pain of my hands, soon desisted. Instead, I lay back and reviewed my position : I was a long way from land ; my hands were burnt, and so, judging from the pain of the sun, was my face ; it was unlikely that anyone on shore had seen me come down and even more unlikely that a ship would come by ; I could float for possibly four hours in my Mae West. I began to feel that I had perhaps been premature in considering myself lucky to have escaped from the machine. After about half an hour my teeth started chattering, and to quiet them I kept up a regular tune-less chant, varying it from time to time with calls for help. There can be few more futile pastimes than yelling for help alone in the North Sea, with a solitary seagull for company, yet it gave me a certain melancholy satisfaction, for I had once written a short story in which the hero (falling from a liner) had done just this. It was rejected.

The water now seemed much colder and I noticed

with surprise that the sun had gone in though my face was still burning. I looked down at my hands, and not seeing them, realized that I had gone blind. So I was going to die. It came to me like that — I was going to die, and I was not afraid. This realization came as a surprise. The manner of my approaching death appalled and horrified me, but the actual vision of death left me unafraid : I felt only a profound curiosity and a sense of satisfaction that within a few minutes or a few hours I was to learn the great answer. I decided that it should be in a few minutes. I had no qualms about hastening my end and, reaching up, I managed to unscrew the valve of my Mae West. The air escaped in a rush and my head went under water. It is said by people who have all but died in the sea that drowning is a pleasant death. I did not find it so. I swallowed a large quantity of water before my head came up again, but derived little satisfaction from it. I tried again, to find that I could not get my face under. I was so enmeshed in my parachute that I could not move. For the next ten minutes, I tore my hands to ribbons on the spring-release catch. It was stuck fast. I lay back exhausted, and then I started to laugh. By this time I was probably not entirely normal and I doubt if my laughter was wholly sane, but there was something irresistibly comical in my grand gesture of suicide being so simply thwarted.

Goethe once wrote that no one, unless he had led the full life and realized himself completely, had the right to take his own life. Providence seemed determined that I should not incur the great man's displeasure.

It is often said that a dying man re-lives his whole life in one rapid kaleidoscope. I merely thought gloomily of the Squadron returning, of my mother at home, and of the few people who would miss me. Outside my family, I could count them on the fingers of one hand. What did gratify me enormously was to find that I indulged in no frantic abasements or prayers to the Almighty. It is an old jibe of God-fearing people that the irreligious always change their tune when about to die : I was pleased to think that I was proving them wrong. Because I seemed to be in for an indeterminate period of waiting, I began to feel a terrible loneliness and sought for some means to take my mind off my plight. I took it for granted that I must soon become delirious, and I attempted to hasten the process : I encouraged my mind to wander vaguely and aimlessly, with the result that I did experience a certain peace. But when I forced myself to think of something concrete, I found that I was still only too lucid. I went on shuttling between the two with varying success until I was picked up. I remember as in a dream hearing somebody shout : it seemed so far away and quite unconnected with me. . . .

7

Then willing arms were dragging me over the side ; my parachute was taken off (and with such ease !) ; a brandy flask was pushed between my swollen lips ; a voice said, " O.K., Joe, it's one of ours and still kicking " ; and I was safe. I was neither relieved nor angry : I was past caring.

It was to the Margate lifeboat that I owed my rescue. Watchers on the coast had seen me come down, and for three hours they had been searching for me. Owing to wrong directions, they were just giving up and turning back for land when ironically enough one of them saw my parachute. They were then fifteen miles east of Margate.

While in the water I had been numb and had felt very little pain. Now that I began to thaw out, the agony was such that I could have cried out. The good fellows made me as comfortable as possible, put up some sort of awning to keep the sun from my face, and phoned through for a doctor. It seemed to me to take an eternity to reach shore. I was put into an ambulance and driven rapidly to hospital. Through all this I was quite conscious, though unable to see. At the hospital they cut off my uniform, I gave the requisite information to a nurse about my next of kin, and then, to my infinite relief, felt a hypodermic syringe pushed into my arm.

I can't help feeling that a good epitaph for me at that moment would have been four lines of Verlaine :

## Proem

Quoique sans patrie et sans roi,
Et très brave ne l'étant guère,
J'ai voulu mourir à la guerre.
La mort n'a pas voulu de moi.

The foundations of an experience of which this crash was, if not the climax, at least the turning point were laid in Oxford before the war.

BOOK ONE

BOOK ONE

# I

## Under the Munich Umbrella

OXFORD has been called many names, from "the city of beautiful nonsense" to "an organized waste of time," and it is characteristic of the place that the harsher names have usually been the inventions of the University's own undergraduates. I had been there two years and was not yet twenty-one when the war broke out. No one could say that we were, in my years, strictly "politically minded." At the same time it would be false to suggest that the University was blissfully unaware of impending disaster. True, one could enter anybody's rooms and within two minutes be engaged in a heated discussion over orthodox versus Fairbairn rowing, or whether Ezra Pound or T. S. Eliot was the daddy of contemporary poetry, while an impassioned harangue on liberty would be received in embarrassed silence. Nevertheless, politics filled a large space. That humorous tradition of Oxford verbosity, the Union, held a political debate every week ; Conservative, Labour, and even Liberal clubs flourished ; and the British Union of Fascists had managed to raise a back-room and twenty-four members.

But it was not to the political societies and meetings that one could look for a representative view of the pre-war undergraduate. Perhaps as good a cross-section of opinion and sentiment as any at Oxford was to be found in Trinity, the college where I spent those two years rowing a great deal, flying a little — I was a member of the University Air Squadron — and reading somewhat.

We were a small college of less than two hundred, but a successful one. We had the president of the Rugby Club, the secretary of the Boat Club, numerous golf, hockey, and running Blues and the best cricketer in the University. We also numbered among us the president of the Dramatic Society, the editor of the *Isis* (the University magazine), and a small but select band of scholars. The sentiment of the college was undoubtedly governed by the more athletic undergraduates, and we radiated an atmosphere of alert Philistinism. Apart from the scholars, we had come up from the so-called better public schools, from Eton, Shrewsbury, Wellington, and Winchester, and while not the richest representatives of the University, we were most of us comfortably enough off. Trinity was, in fact, a typical incubator of the English ruling classes before the war. Most of those with Blues were intelligent enough to get second-class honours in whatever subject they were " reading," and could thus

ensure themselves entry into some branch of the Civil
or Colonial Service, unless they happened to be reading Law, in which case they were sure to have sufficient
private means to go through the lean years of a be-
ginner's career at the Bar or in politics. We were
held together by a common taste in friends, sport,
literature, and idle amusement, by a deep-rooted
distrust of all organized emotion and standardized
patriotism, and by a somewhat self-conscious satisfaction in our ability to succeed without apparent
effort. I went up for my first term, determined,
without over-exertion, to row myself into the Government of the Sudan, that country of blacks ruled by
Blues in which my father had spent so many years.
To our scholars (except the Etonians) we scarcely
spoke ; not, I think, from plain snobbishness, but
because we found we did not speak the same language.
Through force of circumstance they had to work
hard ; they had neither the time nor the money to
cultivate the dilettante browsing which we affected.
As a result they tended to be martial in their en-
thusiasms, whether pacifistic or patriotic. They were
earnest, technically knowing, and conversationally
uninteresting.

Not that conversationally Trinity had any great
claim to distinction. To speak brilliantly was not to
be accepted at once as indispensable ; indeed it might
prove a handicap, giving rise to suspicions of artiness.

It would be tolerated as an idiosyncrasy because of one's prowess at golf, cricket, or some other college sport that proved one's all-rightness. For while one might be clever, on no account must one be unconventional or disturbing — above all disturbing. The scholars' conversation might well have been disturbing. Their very presence gave one the uneasy suspicion that in even so small a community as this while one half thought the world was their oyster, the other half knew it was not and never could be. Our attitude will doubtless strike the reader as reprehensible and snobbish, but I believe it to have been basically a suspicion of anything radical — any change, and not a matter of class distinction. For a man from any walk of life, were he athletic rather than aesthetic, was accepted by the college at once, if he was a decent sort of fellow. Snobbish or not, our attitude was essentially English.

Let us say, therefore, that it was an unconscious appreciation of the simple things of life, an instinctive distrust of any form of adopted aestheticism as insincere.

We had in Trinity several clubs and societies of which, typically, the Dining Club was the most exclusive and the Debating Society the most puerile. Outside the college, the clubs to which we belonged were mostly of a sporting nature, for though some of us in our first year had joined political societies, our enthusiasm soon waned. As for the Union, though we were at first impressed by its great past, and prepared to be amused and possibly instructed by its discussions, we were soon convinced of its fatuity, which exceeded that of the average school debating society.

It was often said that the President of Trinity would accept no one as a Commoner in his college who was not a landowner. This was an exaggeration, but one which the dons were not unwilling to foster. Noel Agazarian, an Armenian friend of mine in another college, once told me that he had been proposed for Trinity, but that the President had written back to his head master regretting that the College could not accept Mr. Agazarian, and pointing out that in 1911, when the last coloured gentleman had been at Trinity, it had really proved most unfortunate.

We were cliquy, extremely limited in our horizon, quite conscious of the fact, and in no way dissatisfied about it. We knew that war was imminent. There was nothing we could do about it. We were depressed by a sense of its inevitability but we were not patriotic. While lacking any political training, we were convinced that we had been needlessly led into the present world crisis, not by unscrupulous rogues, but worse, by the bungling of a crowd of incompetent old fools. We hoped merely that when war came it might be fought with a maximum of individuality and a minimum of discipline.

Though still outwardly complacent and successful, there was a very definite undercurrent of dissatisfaction and frustration amongst nearly everyone I knew during my last year.

Frank Waldron had rowed No. 6 in the Oxford Crew. He stood six-foot-three and had an impressive mass of snow-white hair. Frank was not unintelligent and he was popular. In my first year he had been president of the Junior Common Room. The girls pursued him but he affected to prefer drink. In point of fact he was unsure of himself and was searching for someone to put on a pedestal. He had great personality and an undeveloped character. Apart from myself, he was the laziest though most stylish oarsman in the University, but he was just that much better to get away with it. He did a minimum of work, knowing that it was essential to get a second if he wished to enter the Civil Service, but always finding some plausible argument to convince himself that the various distractions of life were necessities.

I mention Frank here, because, though a caricature, he was in a way representative of a large number of similarly situated young men. He had many unconscious imitators who, because they had not the same prowess or personality, showed up as the drifting shadows that they were.

The seed of self-destruction among the more intellectual members of the University was even more evident. Despising the middle-class society to which they owed their education and position, they attacked it, not with vigour but with an adolescent petulance. They were encouraged in this by their literary idols, by their unquestioning allegiance to Auden, Isherwood, Spender, and Day Lewis. With them they affected a dilettante political leaning to the left. Thus, while refusing to be confined by the limited outlook of their own class, they were regarded with suspicion by the practical exponents of labour as bourgeois, idealistic, pink in their politics and pale-grey in their effectiveness. They balanced precariously and with irritability between a despised world they had come out of and a despising world they couldn't get into. The result, in both their behaviour and their writing, was an inevitable concentration on self, a turning-in on themselves, a breaking-down and not a building-up. To build demanded enthusiasm, and that one could not tolerate. Of this leaning was a friend of mine in another college by the name of David Rutter. He was different not so much in that he was sincere as in that he was a pacifist.

" Modern patriotism," he would say, " is a false emotion. In the Middle Ages they had the right idea. All that a man cared about was his family and his own home on the village green. It was immaterial to him who was ruling the country and what political opinions held sway. Wars were no concern of his." His favourite quotation was the remark of Joan's father in Schiller's drama on the Maid of Orleans, " *Lasst uns still gehorchend harren wem uns Gott zum König gibt,*" which he would translate for me as, " Let us trust obediently in the king God sends us."

" Then," he would go on, " came the industrial revolution. People had to move to the cities. They ceased to live on the land. Meanwhile our country, by being slightly more unscrupulous than anyone else, was obtaining colonies all over the world. Later came the popular press, and we have been exhorted ever since to love not only our own country, but vast tracts of land and people in the Empire whom we have never seen and never wish to see."

I would then ask him to explain the emotion one always feels when, after a long time abroad, the South Coast express steams into Victoria Station. " False, quite false," he would say ; " you're a sentimentalist." I was inclined to agree with him. " Furthermore," he would say, " when this war comes, which, thanks to the benighted muddling of our Government, come it must, whose war is it going to be ? You can't tell me that it will be the same war for the unemployed labourer as for the Duke of Westminster. What are the people to gain from it ? Nothing ! "

But though his arguments against patriotism were

intellectual, his pacifism was emotional. He had a completely sincere hatred of violence and killing, and the spectacle of army chaplains wearing field boots under the surplice revolted him.

At this time I was stroking one of the trial crews for the Oxford boat just previous to being thrown out for "lack of enthusiasm and co-operation." I was also on the editorial staff of the University magazine. David Rutter once asked me how I could reconcile heartiness with aestheticism in my nature. "You're like a man who hires two taxis and runs between," he said. "What are you going to do when the war comes?"

I told him that as I was already in the University Air Squadron I should of course join the Air Force. "In the first place," I said, "I shall get paid and have good food. Secondly, I have none of your sentiments about killing, much as I admire them. In a fighter plane, I believe, we have found a way to return to war as it ought to be, war which is individual combat between two people, in which one either kills or is killed. It's exciting, it's individual, and it's disinterested. I shan't be sitting behind a long-range gun working out how to kill people sixty miles away. I shan't get maimed: either I shall get killed or I shall get a few pleasant putty medals and enjoy being stared at in a night club. Your unfortunate convictions, worthy as they are, will get you at best a few white feathers, and at worst locked up."

"Thank God," said David, "that I at least have the courage of my convictions."

I said nothing, but secretly I admired him. I was by now in a difficult position. I no longer wished to go to the Sudan; I wished to write; but to stop rowing and take to hard work when so near a Blue seemed absurd. Now in France or Germany one may announce at an early age that one intends to write, and one's family reconciles itself to the idea, if not with enthusiasm at least with encouragement. Not so in England. To impress writing as a career on one's parents one must be specific. I was. I announced my intention of becoming a journalist. My family was sceptical, my mother maintaining that I could never bring myself to live on thirty shillings a week, which seemed to her my probable salary for many years to come, while my father seemed to feel that I was in need of a healthier occupation. But my mind was made up. I could not see myself as an empire-builder and I managed to become sports editor of the University magazine. I dared not let myself consider the years out of my life, first at school, and now at the University, which had been sweated away upon the river, earnestly peering one way and going the other. Unfortunately, rowing was the only accomplishment in which I could get credit for being slightly better than average. I was in a dilemma, but I need not have worried. My state of mind was not conducive to good oarsmanship and I was removed from the crew. This at once irritated me and I made efforts to get back, succeeding only in wasting an equal amount of time and energy in the second crew for a lesser amount of glory.

Mentally, too, I felt restricted. It was not intellectual snobbery, but I felt the need sometimes to eat, drink, and think something else than rowing. I had a number of intelligent and witty friends ; but a permanent oarsman's residence at either Putney or Henley gave me small opportunity to enjoy their company. Further, the more my training helped my mechanical perfection as an oarsman, the more it deadened my mind to an appreciation of anything but red meat and a comfortable bed. I made a determined effort to spend more time on the paper, and as a result did no reading for my degree. Had the war not broken, I fear I should have made a poor showing in my finals. This did not particularly worry me, as a degree seemed to me the least important of the University's offerings. Had I not been chained to my oar, I should have undoubtedly read more, though not, I think, for my degree. As it was, I read fairly widely, and, more important, learned a certain *savoir-faire* ; learned how much I could drink, how not to be *gauche* with women, how to talk to people without being aggressive or embarrassed, and gained a measure of confidence which would have been impossible for me under any other form of education.

I had the further advantage of having travelled. When very young I had lived abroad, and every vacation from school and the University I had utilized to visit the Continent. It is maintained by some that travel has no educational value, that a person with sensibility can gain as rich an experience of life by staying right where he is as by wandering around the world, and that a person with no sensibility may as well remain at home anyway. To me this is nonsense, for if one is a bore, I maintain that it is better to be a bore about Peshawar than Upper Tooting. I was more fortunate than some of my friends, for I knew enough French and German to be able to move about alone ; whereas my friends, though they were not insular, tended to travel in organized groups, either to Switzerland for ski-ing in winter or to Austria for camping in summer.

It was on one of these organized trips that Frank Waldron and I went to Germany and Hungary shortly before the war. Frank was no keener on organized groups than I, but we both felt the urge to travel abroad again before it was too late, and we had worked out the cheapest way of doing so. We wrote to the German and Hungarian Governments expressing the hope that we might be allowed to row in their respective countries. They replied that they would be delighted, sent us the times of their regattas (which we very well knew), and expressed the wish that they might be allowed to pay our expenses. We wrote back with appropriate surprise and gratification, and having collected eight others, on July 3, 1938, we set forth.

Half of us went by car and half by train, but we contrived somehow to arrive in Bad Ems together, two days before the race. We were to row for General Goering's Prize Fours. They had originally been the Kaiser Fours, and the gallant General had taken them over.

We left our things at the hotel where we were to stay and took a look at the town which, with its mass of green trees rising in a sheer sweep on either side of the river, made an enchanting picture. Down at the boathouse we had our first encounter with Popeye. He was the local coach and had been a sergeant-major in the last war. With his squat muscled body, his toothless mouth sucking a pipe, the inevitable cap over one eye, his identity was beyond dispute. Popeye was to prove our one invaluable ally. He was very proud of his English though we never discovered where he learned it. After expressing a horrified surprise that we had not brought our own boat, he was full of ideas for helping us.

"Mr. Waldron," he said, "I fix you right up

tomorrow this afternoon. You see, I get you boat."

The next day saw the arrival of several very serious-looking crews and a host of supporters, but no boat. Again we went to Popeye.

" Ah, gentlemen," he said. " My wife, she drunk since two years but tomorrow she come."

We hoped he meant the boat. Fortunately he did, and while leaky and low in the water, it was still a boat and we were mighty relieved to see it. By this time we were regarded with contemptuous amusement by the elegantly turned-out German crews. They came with car-loads of supporters and set, determined faces. Shortly before the race we walked down to the changing-rooms to get ready. All five German crews were lying flat on their backs on mattresses, great brown stupid-looking giants, taking deep breaths. It was all very impressive. I was getting out of my shirt when one of them came up and spoke to me, or rather harangued me, for I had no chance to say anything. He had been watching us, he said, and could only come to the conclusion that we were thoroughly representative of a decadent race. No German crew would dream of appearing so lackadaisical if rowing in England : they would train and they would win. Losing this race might not appear very important to us, but I could rest assured that the German people would not fail to notice and learn from our defeat.

I suggested that it might be advisable to wait until

after the race before shooting his mouth off, but he was not listening. It was Popeye who finally silenced him by announcing that we would win. This caused a roar of laughter and everyone was happy again. As Popeye was our one and only supporter, we taught him to shout " You got to go, boys, you got to go." He assured us that we would hear him.

Looking back, this race was really a surprisingly accurate pointer to the course of the war. We were quite untrained, lacked any form of organization and were really quite hopelessly casual. We even arrived late at the start, where all five German crews were lined up, eager to go. It was explained to us that we would be started in the usual manner ; the starter would call out " Are you ready ? " and if nobody shouted or raised his hand he would fire a gun and we would be off. We made it clear that we understood and came forward expectantly. " Are you ready ? " called the starter. Beside us there was a flurry of oars and all five German crews were several lengths up the river. We got off to a very shaky start and I can't ever remember hearing that gun fired. The car-loads of German supporters were driving slowly along either bank yelling out encouragement to their respective crews in a regulated chant while we rowed in silence, till about quarter-way up the course and above all the roaring and shouting on the banks I heard Popeye : " You got to go, boys, you got to go. All my dough she is on you." I looked up to see Popeye hanging from a branch on the side of the river, his anxious face almost touching the water. When Frank took one hand off his oar and waved to him, I really thought the little man was going to fall in. As we came up to the bridge that was the half-way mark we must have been five lengths behind ; but it was at that moment that somebody spat on us. It was a tactical error. Sammy Stockton, who was stroking the boat, took us up the next half of the course as though pursued by all the fiends in hell and we won the race by two-fifths of a second. General Goering had to surrender his cup and we took it back with us to England. It was a gold shell-case mounted with the German eagle and disgraced our rooms in Oxford for nearly a year until we could stand it no longer and sent it back through the German Embassy. I always regret that we didn't put it to the use which its shape suggested. It was certainly an unpopular win. Had we shown any sort of enthusiasm or given any impression that we had trained they would have tolerated it, but as it was they showed merely a sullen resentment.

Two days later we went on to Budapest. Popeye, faithful to the end, collected a dog-cart and took all our luggage to the station. We shook the old man's hand and thanked him for all he had done.

"Promise me one thing, Popeye," said Frank,

" when the war comes you won't shoot any of us."

" Ah, Mr. Waldron," he replied, " you must not joke of these things. I never shoot you, we are brothers. It is those Frenchies we must shoot. The Tommies, they are good fellows, I remember. We must never fight again."

As the train drew out of the station he stood, a tiny stocky figure, waving his cap until we finally steamed round the bend. We wrote to him later, but he never replied.

We were greeted at Budapest by a delegation. As I stepped on to the platform, a grey-haired man came forward and shook my hand.

" My dear sir," he said, " we are very happy to welcome you to our country. Good-bye."

" Good-bye," I said, introducing him rapidly to the others, half of whom were already climbing back into the train.

We were put up at the Palatinus Hotel on St. Margaret's Island where Frank's antiquated Alvis created a sensation. Members of our party had been dropping off all the way across Europe and it was only by a constant stream of cables and a large measure of luck that we finally mustered eight people in Budapest, where we found to our horror that we had been billed all over town as the Oxford University Crew. Our frame of mind was not improved by the discovery that we had two eights races in the same day, the length of the Henley course, and that we were to be opposed by four Olympic crews. It was so hot it was only possible to row very early in the morning or in the cool of the evening. The Hungarians made sure we had so many official dinners that evening rowing was impossible, and the food was so good and the wines so potent that early-morning exercise was out of the question. Further, the Danube, far from being blue, turned out to be a turbulent brown torrent that made the Tideway seem like a mill-pond in comparison. Out in midstream half-naked giants, leaning over the side of anchored barges, hung on to the rudder to prevent us being carried off downstream before the start. We had to keep our blades above the water until they let go for fear that the stream would tear them out of our hands. Then at the last moment, Sammy Stockton, the one member of our rather temperamental crew who could be relied upon never to show any temperament, turned pale-green. A combination of heat, goulash, and Tokay had proved too much for him and he came up to the start a very sick man. Once again we were pinning all our faith on our Four, as the eight in the bows had an air of uncoordinated individualism. We were three-quarters of the way down the course and still in front, when John Garton, who was steering, ran into the boat on our left. There was an immediate uproar of which we understood not one word, but it was, alas, impossible to misconstrue the meaning of the umpire's arm pointing firmly back towards the start. Once again we battled upstream and turned around with a sense of foreboding. Again we were off, half-way down the course and still ahead : a faint hope began to flutter in my agonized stomach, but it was not to be. The spirit was willing but the flesh was weak. Behind me I heard Sammy let out a whistling sigh like a pricked balloon and the race was over. The jubilation of the Hungarians was tempered by the fact that our defeat nearly caused a crisis, for at the Mayor's banquet that night we were to be presented with medals struck in honour of our victory, and it was doubtful whether any others could be manufactured in time. But they were. The evening passed off admirably. Frank rose to his feet and delivered a speech in fluent if ungrammatical German. He congratulated the Hungarians on their victory, apologized for, but did not excuse our defeat and thanked them for their excellent hospitality. There were, fortunately, no repercussions apart from a cartoon in the *Pesti Hirlap*, showing eight people in a boat looking over their left shoulders at a naked girl in a skiff with the caption underneath : " Why Oxford Lost ? "

The others returned to England shortly afterwards, but I stayed on an extra month with some people I knew who had an estate at Vecses about twelve miles out of Budapest. They were Jews, and even then

very careful about holding large parties or being in
any way publicized for fear of giving a handle to the
Nazi sympathizers in the Government. With them I
travelled all around Hungary and found everywhere
an atmosphere of medieval feudalism : most of the
small towns and villages were peopled entirely by
peasants, apart from a bored army garrison. In
Budapest there was a sincere liking for the English
tempered by an ever-present memory of the Treaty
of Trianon, and a very genuine dislike of the Germans ;
but there was a general resignation to the inevitability
of a Nazi alliance for geographical reasons. Any
suggestion that there was still time for a United
Balkans to put up a solid front as a counter to German
influence was waved aside. The Hungarians were a
proud race ; what had they in common with the
upstart barbarians who surrounded them and who
had so cynically carved up their country ?

I left with a genuine regret and advice from the
British Embassy not to leave the train anywhere on
the way through Germany.

Before the outbreak of the war I made two more
trips abroad, each to France. As soon as I got back
from Hungary I collected the car and motored through
Brittany. My main object was, I must admit, food.
I saw before me possibly years of cold mutton, boiled
potatoes, and Brussels sprouts, and the lure of one
final diet of cognac at fourpence a glass, oysters,

coq-au-vin, and soufflés drew me like a magnet. I motored out through Abbeville, Rouen, Rennes, and Quimper and ended up at Beg Meil, a small fishing village on the east coast, where between rich meals of impossible cheapness and nights of indigestion and remorse I talked with the people. Everywhere there was the same resignation, the same it's-on-the-way-but-what-the-hell attitude. I was in Rouen on the night of Hitler's final speech before Munich. The hysterical " *Sieg Heils !* " of his audience were picked up by the loud-speakers through the streets, and sounded strangely unreal in the quiet evening of the cathedral city. The French said nothing, merely listening in silence and then dispersing with a shrug of their shoulders. The walls were plastered with calling-up notices and the stations crowded with uniforms. There was no excitement. It was as though a very tired old man was bestirring himself for a long-expected and unwelcome appointment.

I got back to England on the day of the Munich Conference ; the boat was crowded and several cars were broken as they were hauled on board. The French seemed to resent our going.

During " peace in our time " I made my final trip. The Oxford and Cambridge crews were invited to Cannes to row on the bay and I had the enviable position of spare man. Café society was there in force ; there were fireworks, banquets at Juan-les-

Pins, battles of flowers at Nice, and a general air of all being for the best in the best of all possible worlds. We stayed at the Carlton, bathed at Eden Rock and spent most of the night in the Casino. We gave a dinner for the Mayor which ended with Frank and the guest of honour rolled together in the tablecloth singing quite unintelligible ditties, much to the surprise of the more sober diners. We emerged from some night club at seven o'clock on the morning of our departure with a bare half-hour left to catch our plane. Over the doorway a Union Jack and a Tricolour embraced each other in a rather tired entente cordiale. Frank seized the Tricolour and waved it gaily above his head. At that moment the smallest Frenchman I've ever seen rushed after us and clutched hold of Frank's retreating coat-tails.

" *Mais, non, non, non !* " he screeched.

" *Mais, oui, oui, oui,* my little man," said Frank, and, disengaging himself, he belaboured the fellow over the head with the emblem of his Fatherland and cantered off down the road, to appear twenty minutes later on the airport, a sponge bag in one hand and the Tricolour still firmly clasped in the other.

This, then, was the Oxford Generation which on September 3, 1939, went to war. I have of necessity described that part of the University with which I came in contact and which was particularly self-sufficient, but I venture to think that we differed little in essentials from the majority of young men with a similar education. We were disillusioned and spoiled. The press referred to us as the Lost Generation and we were not displeased. Superficially we were selfish and egocentric without any Holy Grail in which we could lose ourselves. The war provided it, and in a delightfully palatable form. It demanded no heroics, but gave us the opportunity to demonstrate in action our dislike of organized emotion and patriotism, the opportunity to prove to ourselves and to the world that our effete veneer was not as deep as our dislike of interference, the opportunity to prove that, undisciplined though we might be, we were a match for Hitler's dogma-fed youth.

For myself, I was glad for purely selfish reasons. The war solved all problems of a career, and promised a chance of self-realization that would normally take years to achieve. As a fighter pilot I hoped for a concentration of amusement, fear, and exaltation which it would be impossible to experience in any other form of existence.

I was not disappointed.

September 3, 1939, fell during the long vacation, and all of us in the University Air Squadron reported that day to the Volunteer Reserve Centre at Oxford. I drove up from Beaconsfield in the late afternoon and discovered with the rest that we had made a mistake : the radio calling-up notice had referred only to ground crews and not to pilots. Instead of going home, I went along with Frank to his old rooms and we settled down to while away the evening.

Frank was then twenty-five and had just finished his last year. We had both rowed more than we had flown, and would have a lot to learn about flying. The walls of Frank's rooms were covered with oars, old prints, and the photographs of one or two actresses whom we had known : outside there was black-out and the noise of marching feet. We said little. Through that window there came to us, with an impact that was a shock, a breath of the new life we were to be hurled into. There was a heavy silence in the air that was ominous. I was moved, full of new and rather awed emotions. I wanted to say something but could not. I felt a curious constraint. At that moment there was a loud banging on the door, and we started up. Outside stood a policeman. We knew him well.

" I might have known," he said, " that it would be you two."

" Good evening, Rogers," said Frank. " Surely no complaints. Term hasn't begun yet."

" No, Mr. Waldron, but the war has. Just take a look at your window."

We looked up. A brilliant shaft of light was illuminating the street for fifty yards on either side of the house. Not a very auspicious start to our war careers.

## 2

## *Before Dunkirk*

FOR some time we reported regularly every fortnight to the Air Centre at Oxford, where we were paid a handsome sum of money and told to stand by. Then we were drafted to an Initial Training Wing. We were marched from the station to various colleges and I found myself supplied with a straw bed and command of a platoon. My fellow sergeants were certainly tough : they were farmers, bank clerks, estate agents, representatives of every class and calling, and just about the nicest bunch of men it has ever been my lot to meet. There could have been few people less fitted to drill them than I, but by a system of the majority vote we overcame most of our difficulties. If ignorant of on what foot to give a command, I would have a stand-easy and take a show of hands. The idea worked admirably and whenever an officer appeared our platoon was a model of efficiency. We never saw an aeroplane and seldom attended a lecture. This was the pre-Dunkirk "phoney war" period, but life was not dull. Soon afterwards I was commissioned on the score of my proficiency certificate in the University Air Squadron, and was moved to another Wing. Here I found myself amongst many old friends.

Frank Waldron was there, Noel Agazarian, and Michael Judd, also of the University Squadron. Michael thought and felt as egocentrically as I did about everything, but his reaction to the war was different. It did not fit into his plans, for he had just won a travelling fellowship at All Souls : to him the war was in fact a confounded nuisance. Although we were officers, route marches were nevertheless obligatory for us ; but by some odd chance Frank and Noel and I always seemed to be in the last section of threes on the march. Prominent and eager at the start, we were somehow never to be seen by the end. London, I fear, accounted for more than enough of our time and money. That our behaviour was odd and uncooperative did not occur to us, or if it did, caused us few pangs. We had joined the Air Force to fly, and not to parade around like Boy Scouts. We didn't bother to consider that elementary training might be as essential as anything that we should learn later, or that a certain confusion of organization was inevitable at the beginning of the war. We rented a large room in a hotel and formed a club, pleasantly idling away six weeks in drinking and playing cards.

Then one day it was announced that we were to

move. The news was greeted with enthusiasm, for while the prospect of flying seemed no nearer, this station was notoriously gay and seemed a step in the right direction. There had been pictures in the press of young men diving into the swimming-pool, of Mr. Wally Hammond leading a parade, and of Len Harvey and Eddie Phillips boxing. David Douglas-Hamilton, who boxed for England, and Noel, who boxed for Oxford, were particularly pleased.

I drove down with Frank in his battered old Alvis and reported. We were billeted in boarding-houses along the front. I had never quite believed in the legend of seaside boarding-houses, but within two days I was convinced. There it all was, the heavy smell of Brussels sprouts, the aspidistras, the slut of a maid with a hole in her black stockings and a filthy thumb-nail in the soup, the communal table in the dining-room which just didn't face the sea, the two meals a day served punctually at one o'clock and seven-thirty.

We found that Nigel Bicknell, Bill Aitken, and Dick Holdsworth had been billeted in the same boarding-house. The way in which they took the war deserves to be mentioned.

Nigel was a year or two older than I. He had been editor of the *Granta*, the University magazine at Cambridge. From Nigel's behaviour, referred to a little later, it will be seen that the attitude of Cambridge to the war was the same as ours. He had had a tentative job on the *Daily Express*, and by the outbreak of the war he had laid the foundations of a career. For him as for Michael Judd, the war was a confounded nuisance.

Bill Aitken was older. He had the Beaverbrook forehead and directness of approach. He was director of several companies, married, and with considerably more to lose by joining the R.A.F. as a pilot officer than any of us. The immediate pettiness of our regulations and our momentary inactivity brought from him none of the petulant outbursts in which most of us indulged, nor did he display the same absorption with himself and what he was to get out of it.

Dick Holdsworth had much the same attitude. He was to me that nothing short of miraculous combination, a First in Law and a rowing Blue. He too was several years older than most of us and considerably better orientated : his good-natured compliance with the most child-like rules and determined eagerness to gain everything possible from the Course ensured him the respect of our instructors. But the others were mostly of my age and it was with no very good grace that we submitted to a fortnight's pep course.

We went for no more route marches, but drilled vigorously on the pier ; we had no lectures on flying but several on deportment ; we were told to get our hair cut and told of the importance of forming threes for the proper handling of an aircraft ; but of the sporting celebrities we were told nothing and saw little, until after much pleading a boxing tournament was arranged. Noel and David both acquitted themselves well, David hitting Len Harvey harder and more often than the champion expected. We applauded with suitable enthusiasm, and marched back to the pier for more drill.

At the end of a fortnight our postings to flying training schools came through and our period of inactivity was over. Dick Holdsworth, Noel, Peter Howes, and I were to report at a small village on the north-east coast of Scotland. None of us had ever heard of it, but none of us cared : as long as we flew it was immaterial to us where. As we were likely to be together for some months to come, I was relieved to be going with people whom I both knew and liked. Noel, with his pleasantly ugly face, had been sent down from Oxford over a slight matter of breaking up his college and intended reading for the Bar. With an Armenian father and a French mother he was by nature cosmopolitan, intelligent, and a brilliant linguist, but an English education had discovered that he was an athlete, and his University triumphs had been of brawn rather than brain. Of this he was very well aware and somewhat bewildered by it. These warring elements in his make-up made him a most amusing companion and a very good friend. Peter Howes, lanky and of cadaverous good looks, had been reading for a science degree. With a permanently harassed expression on his face he could be a good talker, and was never so happy as when, lying back smoking his pipe, he could expound his theories on sex (of which he knew very little), on literature (of which he knew more), and on mathematics (of which he knew a great deal). He was to prove an invaluable asset in our Wings Exam.

Peter, Noel, and I drove up together. We arrived in the late afternoon of a raw, cold November day. When we had reported to the Station Adjutant, Peter drove us down to the little greystone house in the neighbouring village that was to be our home for many months. Our landlady, a somewhat bewildered old body, showed us with pride the room in which we were to sleep. It was cold and without heating. The iron bedsteads stood austerely in the middle of the room, and an enamelled wash-basin stood in the corner. An old print hung by the window, and a bewhiskered ancestor looked stonily at us from over the wash-stand. The room was scrupulously clean. We assured her that we should be most comfortable, and returned, a little chastened, to the camp.

At the beginning of the war there was a definite prejudice in the Air Force against Volunteer Reserve Officers, and we had the added disadvantage of an

Oxford attitude to life. We were expected to be superior; we were known as week-end pilots; we were known as the long-haired boys; we were to have the nonsense knocked out of us. When I say "we" I don't include Dick Holdsworth. He settled down at once and was perfectly content: he was obviously willing to cooperate to the full. Noel, Peter, and I, less mature and more assertive, looked for trouble and found it. It came in the form of the Chief Ground Instructor, who took to his task of settling our hash with enthusiasm; but our innate laziness added to a certain low cunning proved equal to the situation, and we managed to skip quite a number of morning parades and lectures. There admittedly can be no excuse for our behaviour, but there is, I think, an explanation, to be found in the fact that Dunkirk had not come: the war was still one of tin soldiers and not yet of reality. Nevertheless, thanks to the fact that we got on well with our co-pilots, and to Noel's infectious good-humour and lack of affectation, we gradually settled down to a harmonious relationship with our instructors, who were willing enough to help as soon as we showed signs of cooperation. Our lives quickly became a regular routine of flying and lectures. Dick Holdsworth started in on bombing training, but through making a nuisance of ourselves we three managed to fly Harvards, American fighter trainers.

In our flying instructors Noel and I were very lucky. Noel was handed over to Sergeant Robinson, I to Sergeant White. They were great friends, and a rivalry immediately began to see who could first make a pilot out of the unpromising material that we represented. White was a dour, taciturn little Scot with a dry sense of humour. I liked him at once.

Noel's flying was typical of the man : rough, slap-dash, and with touches of brilliance. Owing to the complete blank in my mind on the subject of anything mechanical, I was at first bewildered by the complicated array of knobs and buttons confronting me in the cockpit. I was convinced that I might at any moment haul up the under-carriage while still on the ground, or switch off the engine in the air, out of pure confusion of mind. However, thanks to the patience and consideration of Sergeant White, I developed gradually from a mediocre performer to a quite moderate pilot. For weeks he sat behind me in the rear cockpit muttering, just loud enough for me to hear, about the bad luck of getting such a bum for a pupil. Then one day he called down the Inter-Comm., " Man, you can fly at last. Now I want you to dust the pants of Agazarian and show our friend, Sergeant Robinson, that he's not the only one with a pupil that's not a half-wit."

My recollection of our Scottish training is a con-fusion of, in the main, pleasant memories : Of my first solo cross-country flight, when I nearly made a forced landing down-wind in a field with a large white house at the far end. A little red light inside the cockpit started winking at me, and then the engine cut. The red light continued to shine like a brothel invitation while I racked my brain to think what was wrong. I was down to 500 feet, and more frightened of making a fool of myself than of crashing, when I remembered. It was the warning signal for no petrol. I quickly changed tanks, grateful that there were no spectators of my stupidity, and flew back, determined to learn my cockpit drill thoroughly before taking to the air again.

Of my second solo cross-country flight when the engine cut again, this time due to no fault of mine. Both the magnetos were burned out. I was on my way back from Wick and flying at about 2000 feet when the engine spluttered twice and stopped. By the grace of God I was near a small aerodrome backed by a purple range of mountains and opening on to the sea. There was no time to make a circuit, so I banked and, feeling decidedly queasy, put down right across two incoming machines to pull up six yards from the sea.

Of cloud and formation flying. I shall never forget the first time that I flew really high, and, looking down, saw wave after wave of white undulating cloud that stretched for miles in every direction like some fairy city. I dived along a great canyon ; the sun threw the reddish shadow of the plane on to the cotton-wool walls of white cliff that towered up on either side. It was intoxicating. I flew on. Soon I could see nothing and had to rely on my instruments. I did a slow roll. This was extremely stupid apart from being strictly forbidden. My speed fell off alarmingly. I pushed the stick forward : the speed fell still further and I nearly went into a spin. I could not tell whether I was on my back or right way up, and felt very unhappy. I lost about 2000 feet and came out of the cloud in a screaming spiral, but still fortunately a long way above the earth. I straightened up and flew home with another lesson hard learned.

Formation flying was the most popular and exciting part of our training. At first I was very erratic, perilously close to the leader one minute and a quarter of a mile away the next. But gradually I began to improve, and after a few hours I was really enjoying myself. We had a flight commander who, once we were steady, insisted on us flying in very tight formation, the wing-tip of the outside machine in line with the roundel on the leader's fuselage. He was a brave man and it certainly gave us confidence. Landing was a simple ritual of sign language ; undercarriage down, engine into fine pitch, and flaps down, always without taking one's eyes off the leader. There was a tendency to drift away slightly before touching-down, but we invariably landed as close as we dared, even among ourselves, until one day the C.O. of advanced training stood and watched us. I think he nearly had a stroke, and from then on we confined our tight formations to less public parts of the sky.

Of the scenery, which was superb. Many times of an evening I would stand on the shore and look out to sea, where a curious phosphorescent green was changing to a transparent blue. Behind the camp the setting sun, like a flaming ball, painted the mountains purple and gold. The air was like champagne, and as we were in the Gulf Stream the weather was beautifully mild. While violent snowstorms were raging in England, we were enjoying the most perfect flying weather and a day which lasted for nearly twenty-four hours.

On leave for four days, Noel and I drove across Scotland to the west coast and took the ferry over to Skye. The small stone quay was spotted with shops ; a bus was drawn up by the waterside, a hotel advertisement on its side. I looked at Noel and he nodded. We had come prepared to be disappointed. But we had not driven far before the road gave way to a winding track and the only signs of habitation were a few crofters' cottages. It was evening when we drew up outside the Sligachan Inn at the foot of the Coolin mountains. The innkeeper welcomed us and showed us our rooms. From every window was the same view, grey mountains rising in austere beauty, their peaks hidden in a white mist, and everywhere a great feeling of stillness. The shadows that lengthened across the valley, the streams that coursed down the rocks, the thin mist turning now into night, all a part of that stillness. I shivered. Skye was a world that one would either love or hate ; there could be no temporizing.

" It is very beautiful," said the landlord.

" Yes," I said, " it's beautiful."

" But only mountaineers or fools will climb those peaks."

" We're both fools," Noel said shortly.

" So be it. Dinner is at 8.30."

We stood a while at the window. The night was clear and our heads felt clear and cold as the air. We smelled the odour of the ground in the spring after rain and behind us the wood smoke of the pine fire in our room, and we were content. For these are the odours of nostalgia, spring mist and wood smoke, and never the scent of a woman or of food.

We were alone in the inn save for one old man who had returned there to die. His hair was white but his face and bearing were still those of a mountaineer, though he must have been a great age. He never spoke, but appeared regularly at meals to take his place at a table tight-pressed against the window, alone with his wine and his memories. We thought him rather fine.

In the morning we set off early, warmed by a rare spring sun which soon dried the dew from the heather. We had decided on Bruach-na-Free, one of the easier peaks, but it was lunch-time before we reached the base of the first stiff climb and the muscles in our thighs were already taut. We rested and ate our sandwiches and drank from a mountain stream. The water was achingly cold. Then we started to climb. In the morning we had taken our time and talked, now we moved fast and said nothing. With feet and hands we forced our way up the lower grey crumbling rock to the wet black smooth surface, mist-clouded above. There was no friendship in that climb: neither of us had spoken, but each knew that the other meant to reach the top first. Once I slipped and dropped back several feet, cutting open my hand. Noel did not stop ; he did not even turn his head. I would not have forgiven him if he had. Gradually I brought him back. Nothing disturbed that great stillness but the occasional crash of a loose stone and the sobbing of our breath. We were no longer going up and around the face of the mountain but climbing straight. We could see nothing in the mist, but my thigh muscles were twitching with the strain and my arms were on fire. Then I felt a cold breeze blowing down on my upturned face and knew we were near the top. I practically threw myself up the last few yards, but Noel hung on to his advantage and hauled himself

up the last ledge with a gasp of relief, a second or two
before me. We lay on our backs, and felt the black
wet rock cold against us, felt the deep mist damp
against our faces, felt the sweat as it trickled into our
eyes, felt the air in deep gulps within our lungs. The
war was far away and life was very good.

We could see nothing below us, but started off
down, jumping and slithering on the avalanche of
rocks that cascaded beside us, making a great thunder
of noise in that deep stillness. We soon felt again the
sun, warm on our faces, and saw below us the bed of
a mountain stream leading away into the distance,
and scarcely visible, a mere speck at the far end, the
inn. We did not hesitate to follow the stream, as it
was running low, and we made quite good time until
we came to a drop of some twelve feet where the water
fell in a small torrent. This we managed to negotiate
without getting too wet, only to be met a few yards
further on with a sheer drop of some twenty feet.
The stream had become a river and dropped down
into a shallow pool some two feet deep. It was impossible to go back and there was only one way of
going on. "You first," I said to Noel. "Give me your
clothes and I'll throw them down to you with mine."

Now early March is no time for bathing anywhere,
but there can be few colder places that we could have
chosen than the mountain streams of Skye. Noel
stripped, handed me his clothes, and let himself down

as far as possible. Then he let go. He landed on all
fours and scrambled out unhurt, a grotesque white
figure amidst those sombre rocks.

"For Christ's sake hurry up : I'm freezing."

"I'm right with you," I shouted, and then with
Noel's clothes firmly clutched under my arm, and
still wearing my own, I slipped. I had a short glimpse
of Noel's agonized face watching the delicate curve
of one of his shoes through the air and then I was
under the water with two grazed knees. It was
freezingly cold, but I managed to grab everything
and wallowed painfully out.

"You bastard," said Noel.

"I'm sorry, but look at me : I'm just as wet."

"Yes, but you're wearing your clothes : I've got
to put these bloody things on again."

With much muttering he finally got dressed, and
we squelched our way onwards. By the time we
reached the inn two hours later we were dry but
mighty hungry.

Over dinner we told the landlord of our novel
descent. His sole comment was "Humph," but the
old man at the window turned and smiled at us. I
think he approved.

Of crashes. It was after an armament lecture in
one of the huts when we heard, very high, the thin
wailing scream of a plane coming down fast. The
corporal sat down and rolled himself a cigarette. He

took out the paper and made of it a neat trough with his forefinger, opened the tin of tobacco and sprinkled a little on to the paper, ran his tongue along the paper edge and then rolled it. As he put it in his mouth we heard the crash, maybe a mile away. The corporal lit a match and spoke : " I remember the last time we had one of those. I was on the salvage party. It wasn't a pretty sight."

We learned later that the man had been on a warload height test and had presumably fainted. They did not find much of him, but we filled up the coffin with sand and gave him a grand funeral.

And again night flying. It was a dark night, but cloudless. Noel and I walked down together from the Mess. A slight carpet of snow covered the ground and gave an almost fairy-like appearance to the wooden living-huts. Through a chink in the blackout a thin ray of light shone out from one of the windows. A dry wind rustled over the bleakness of the field as we crunched our way across the tarmac and pushed open the door of the hangar.

I pulled on my sidcot and gloves and slipped my feet into the comforting warmth of my fur-lined boots. I was to be off first. Sergeant White strode in smoking a cigarette :

" Well, you couldn't want a better night. Even you shouldn't make a mistake with this carpet on the ground."

" Bet you need more than three dual circuits," said Noel. (He meant three times in with the instructor before I could do it solo.)

I took the bet and we walked out on to the field. I could see the machine, a squat dark patch against the grey of the horizon. I hauled myself up on to the wing, buckled on my parachute harness, and climbed into the front cockpit, while the fitter stood by to strap me in. I settled myself comfortably into the box seat, glanced over the dimly shining instrument panel, and plugged in my ear-phones.

" All set."

" Right, Hillary. Run her up."

I lifted my hand to the rigger and he disappeared. I pulled the stick back into my stomach and gradually opened the throttle, automatically checking engine revs., oil pressure, and temperature. The engine burst forth from a stutter to a great even roar of sound, hurling a scream of defiance into the night. I throttled back, waved away the chocks from under the wheels, and let the machine roll gently forward to the taxiing post.

Across about a hundred yards from us lay the flare path, a straight line of dimly glowing light. The officer in charge of night flying and a sergeant with the Aldis lamp sat huddled in their greatcoats at the near end. There was no landing beacon. I tapped out my letter on the Morse key, had it returned in green by the lamp, and swung the machine into wind. I pushed the throttle wide open and eased the stick forward. As we gathered speed and the flickering lights of the flare path tore past in a confused blur, I knew that I was too tense. I could feel my hand hard-clenched on the control stick. I was swinging into the flare path and I felt White give a slight push on the rudder. The tail came up and then with one slight bump we were off the ground.

Reassuringly came White's voice : " Climb up to a thousand feet and do a normal circuit. Watch your speed."

Automatically as we climbed I hauled up the under-carriage, and pushed the pitch lever into coarse. I straightened out at a thousand feet, and, with my eyes fixed on the turn-and-bank indicator, pushed rudder and stick together to do a gentle turn to the left. Then I looked round me. Below lay the flare path, a thin snake of light, while ahead the sea was shot with silver beneath a sky of studded jewels. I could just make out the horizon and it gave me a feeling of confidence. I relaxed back into my seat, lifted my head from the cockpit, and took a lighter hold of the stick. Behind me I could hear White humming softly. I tapped out my letter and a flash of green answered from the ground. I banked again, and flying down-wind, released the undercarriage : another turn and I changed into fine pitch, throttling back slowly. In the silence that followed turning into the flare path, I saw the lights rushing up to meet us and could feel myself tensing up again.

" Watch your speed now."

" O.K."

We were up to the first flare and I started to ease the stick back.

" Not yet, you're too high."

I felt the pressure on the stick as White continued to hold it forward. We were up to the second flare and still not down. I had a moment of panic. I was going to stall, we were going too fast, couldn't possibly get down, I was making a fool of myself. Then a slight bump, the wheels rumbling along the runway, and White's voice, " Hold her straight, man." We were down.

Twice more we went round before White climbed out and poked his head into the front cockpit : " Think you can take her round yourself, now ? "

" Sure."

" Well, off you go then, and for God's sake don't make a mess of it. I want some sleep tonight."

For the first few minutes I flew automatically, but with a subdued feeling of excitement. Then again I lifted my eyes from the instrument panel and looked for the horizon. I could not see it. Heavy clouds obscured the stars, and outside the dimly lighted cockpit lay pitch darkness. I looked for the flare path and for a moment could not pick it up. I glanced back at the instruments. I was gaining speed rapidly. That meant I was diving. Jerkily I hauled back on the stick. My speed fell off alarmingly. I knew exactly what to do, for I had had plenty of experience in instrument flying ; but for a moment I was paralysed. Enclosed in that small space and faced with a thousand bewildering instruments, I had a moment of complete claustrophobia. I must get out. I was going to crash. I did not know in which direction I was going. Was I even right way up ? I half stood up in my seat. Then I saw the flare path. I was not lost : I was in a perfectly normal position. I dropped back into my seat feeling thoroughly ashamed of myself. The awful feeling of being shut in was gone, and I began to enjoy myself. I was released, filled with a feeling of power, of exaltation. To be up there alone, confident that the machine would answer the least touch on the controls, to be isolated, entirely responsible for one's own return to earth — this was every man's ambition and for a moment I had nearly lost it.

I had to make a couple more circuits before I could get the signal to land. Two machines came in before me. Then I was down, the wheels skimming the ground. I turned off at the end of the flare path and taxied slowly back, swinging the machine gently from side to side. I made my second solo circuit, brought off an adequate landing, and climbed out. White met me as I walked into the hangar.

"O.K.," he said, "you'll do."

We sat down and he handed me a cigarette. Outside someone was coming in to land. He was given a green on the Aldis lamp and throttled back, only to open up and go round again. We watched the glimmer of his navigation lights as he made a quick circuit and once again throttled back. He was past the first flare, past the second, past the third and still not touching down when the engine roared into life and he was off again.

"Christ," said White, "he's in coarse pitch."

Again we watched the navigation lights, but we soon lost them and could just hear the hum of the engine headed towards the sea. Ten minutes went by; twenty minutes. Nobody spoke. Then the officer in charge of night flying walked into the hangar.

"I've sent up for some more airmen. Meanwhile you all spread out and look. Move out to the sea."

"Who was it?" someone asked.

"Ross. Get moving. We don't want to be here all night."

We found him on the shore, the machine half in and half out of the sea. The officer in charge of night flying climbed on to the wing and peered into the cockpit.

"In coarse pitch," he said, "as I thought." Then

after a slight pause, " Poor devil."

I remembered again that moment of blind panic and knew what he must have felt. In his breast pocket was £10, drawn to go on leave the next day. He was twenty years old.

Of people. The other pilots on our Course were a diverse and representative lot. They ranged from schoolboys of eighteen to men of twenty-six. They had taken on their short service commissions, because they were bored with their jobs, sensed the imminence of war, or, amongst the youngest, simply for the joy of flying. To my surprise, I discovered that they nearly all had a familiarity with mechanics and a degree of mathematical perception well ahead of my own. I consoled myself with the thought that I had always despised the mathematical mind and that few great men had possessed one. This was cold comfort ; but what did seem more to the point was that if anything were to go wrong with my engine in mid-air I could hardly climb blithely out on to the wing and mend it. I was cheered to discover that Charlie Frizell, the most competent pilot on the Course, was almost as mathematically imbecile as I. He had, however, an instinct for flying and a certain dash which marked him out as a future fighter pilot. He was nineteen and had joined the Air Force because he wanted a job.

While Charlie Frizell was nineteen and flying

Harvards, Bob Marriott was twenty-six and training for bombers ; yet they had much in common. They were both lazy (we took to them at once) and about as successful at dodging parades and lectures as we. Bob's instructor was the same age as Charlie Frizell, but this age juxtaposition between pupils and instructors was nothing rare and seemed to work out well enough. Then there was Giddings, an ex-school teacher, tall, ungainly, and oppressively serious-minded, who would never appear in the Mess with the others but always retired to his room to pore over his books on navigation and Theory of Flight. There was Benbow, a merchant seaman all his life who had given up freighters for bombers, with an inexhaustible supply of dubious sea stories ; Perkins, once a lawyer in South Africa, small, quiet, monosyllabic, and the soul of courtesy when sober, an unrecognizable glass-chewing trouble-maker when drunk ; Russell, a mustachioed, swashbuckling, would-be leader of men, convinced that he was the best pilot on the Course, but a sound enough fellow underneath. He amused us and mortified himself by landing his Harvard with the undercarriage up, quietly oblivious of the warning hooter inside the machine. Finally, Harry M'Grath and Dixie Dean.

I mention them together, but they could not have been more unlike. Harry, vast, genial, and thirty-two, with a cigarette permanently glued to his lower lip, was married and had a child. He had an Irish temper that flared up and then as quickly changed to shrill trumpetings of elephantine laughter. He had been on the Reserve for some time, having once flown Vickers Virginias. In Ireland before the war he had been in some job connected with Civil Aviation. Dixie, diminutive, desperately keen, and nineteen, with, off duty, the most startling taste in clothes, and shoulders to his suits that you could ski off, was just out of school and adolescing self-consciously all over the place. He was as yet no great performer in the air, but pathetically keen to prove himself. When the others laughed at him, his narrow little face would tighten up with the determination to be the best pilot of them all.

This was a cross-section of the raw material out of which must be welded officers competent to take their place in Fighters, Bombers, and Coastal Command. After the day's work was over we would gather in the Mess or adjourn to some neighbouring pub to pass the evening talking and drinking beer. And there as the months went by one could watch the gradual assimilation of these men, so diverse in their lives and habits, into something bigger than themselves, their integration into the composite figure that is the Air Force Pilot. Unknown to themselves, the realization of all this was gradually instilled in the embryo pilots who lived together, laughing, quarrelling, rapidly maturing in the incubator of that station.

Much that is untrue and misleading has been written on the pilot in this war. Within one short year he has become the nation's hero, and the attempt to live up to this false conception bores him. For, as he would be the first to admit, on the ground the pilot is a very ordinary fellow. Songs such as " Silver Wings " —

> They say he's just a crazy sort of guy,
> But to me he means a million other things,

make him writhe with very genuine embarrassment.

The pilot is of a race of men who since time immemorial have been inarticulate ; who, through their daily contact with death, have realized, often enough unconsciously, certain fundamental things. It is only in the air that the pilot can grasp that feeling, that flash of knowledge, of insight, that matures him beyond his years ; only in the air that he knows suddenly he is a man in a world of men. " Coming back to earth " has for him a double significance. He finds it difficult to orientate himself in a world that is so worldly, amongst a people whose conversation seems to him brilliant, minds agile, and knowledge complete — yet a people somehow blind. It is very strange.

In his village before the war the comfortably-off stockbrokers, the retired officers and business men, thought of the pilot, if they thought of him at all, as rather raffish, not a gentleman. Now they are eager to speak to him, to show him hospitality, to be seen about with him, to tell him that they too are doing their bit. He's a fine fellow, the saviour of the country ; he must have qualities which they had overlooked. But they can't find them. He is polite, but not effusive. They are puzzled and he is embarrassed.

He wants only to get back to the Mess, to be among his own kind, with men who act and don't talk, or if they do, talk only shop ; of old So-and-so and his temper, of flights and crashes, of personal experiences ; bragging with that understatement so dear to the Englishman. He wants to get back to that closed language that is Air Force slang.

These men, who in the air must have their minds clear, their nerves controlled, and their concentration intense, ask on the ground only to be allowed to relax. They ask only to get out of uniform ; in the Mess, to read not literature but thrillers, not *The Times* but the *Daily Mirror*. Indeed Popeye has been adopted by the Air Force. As these men fight the war they have no particular desire to read about it. They like to drink a little beer, play the radio and a little bridge. On leave they want only to get home to their wives and families and be left to themselves.

On some stations officers, if they are married, live out. On others it is forbidden. This depends on the

Commanding Officer, some believing the sudden
change from night-bombing attacks over Berlin to
all the comforts of home to be a psychological error,
others believing it to be beneficial. In most squadrons
the pilots live on the station, going home only on
leave. It is always possible to apply for compassionate
leave in the event of serious domestic trouble, and this
is nearly always granted, though the Passionate Leave
applied for by some Squadrons doesn't receive quite
the same sympathy.

It might be imagined that there would be some
lack of sympathy between the pilots and the ground
staff of an aerodrome, that the pilots would adopt a
rather patronizing manner towards the stores officers,
engineers, signal operators, and adjutants of a station,
rather similar to that condescension shown by the more
highfalutin regiments towards the Royal Army Service
Corps. But this is hardly ever true. On every station
that I know there is an easy comradeship between
pilots and technicians. Each realizes the essential value
of the other — though I must admit on one occasion
hearing a pilot define the height of impertinence as a
stores officer wearing flying boots.

While on duty most pilots drink nothing and
smoke little ; when on leave they welcome the opportunity for an occasional carouse in London. They
get a somewhat malicious pleasure in appearing slightly
scruffy when dining at the smartest restaurants, thus

tending to embarrass the beautifully turned out, pink-and-white-cheeked young men of the crack infantry regiments, and making them feel uncomfortably closely related to chorus boys.

But though these men may seem to fit into the picture of everyday life, though they seem content enough in the company of other men and in the restfulness of their homes, yet they are really only happy when they are back with their Squadrons, with their associations and memories. They long to be back in their planes, so that isolated with the wind and the stars they may play their part in man's struggle against the elements.

The change in Peter Howes was perhaps the most interesting, for he was not unaware of what was happening. From an almost morbid introspection, an unhappy preoccupation with the psychological labyrinths of his own mind, his personality blossomed, like some plant long untouched by the sun, into an at first unwilling but soon open acceptance of the ideas and habits of the others. Peter had a biting tongue when he chose to use it. I remember one night we were discussing Air Force slang and its origins. I started off on some theory but he cut me short. "Nonsense," he said. "You must under-stand that in our service we have a number of unedu-cated louts from all over the world none of whom can speak his own language properly. It thus becomes necessary to invent a small vocabulary of phrases, equipped with which they can carry on together an intelligible conversation." At this time he was a very bad pilot, though his English was meticulous. In three months he was an excellent pilot and his vocabulary was pure R.A.F. I don't know if there is a connection, but I wonder. With enthusiasm he would join in the general debunking when an offender was caught " shooting a line."

Of the war. From time to time without warning a Squadron of long-range bombers would come dropping out of the sky. For a week or so they would make our station their headquarters for raids on Norway, the heavy drone of their engines announcing their return as night began to fall. One day nine set out and four returned. I watched closely the pilots in the Mess that night but their faces were expressionless : they played bridge as usual and discussed the next day's raid.

Then one day a Spitfire Squadron dropped in. It was our first glimpse of the machine which Peter, Noel, and I hoped eventually to fly. The trim deceptive frailty of their lines fascinated us and we spent much of our spare time climbing on to their wings and inspecting the controls. For while we continued to refuse to consider the war in the light of a crusade for humanity, or a life-and-death struggle for civilization, and concerned ourselves merely with what there was in it for us, yet for that very reason we were most anxious to fly single-seater fighters.

The Course drew to a close. We had done a good many hours' flying on service types. We had taken our Wings Examination and somehow managed to pass. Giddings, our ex-schoolmaster, was way out in front, and I, thanks to Peter's knowledge of navigation and Noel's of armament, just scraped through.

We had learned something of flying and the theory of combat, but more important, we had learned a little of how to handle ourselves when we got to our Squadrons. We awaited our final postings with impatience, but their arrival was a bitter disappointment. Only Charlie Frizell and two others were to go into Fighters : at this early stage there had been few casualties in Fighter Command and there was little demand for replacements. Noel, Peter, and I were all slated for Army Co-operation. This entailed further training at Old Sarum before we should finally be operational, operational on Lysanders, machines which Peter gloomily termed " flying coffins." Giddings and a few other good sober pilots were to be instructors ; the remainder were split up between bombers and Coastal Command.

And so we said good-bye to Scotland and headed south.

# 3

## *Spitfires*

NOEL and I spent one night in London. Peter Howes collected us at about ten o'clock and we drove down to Old Sarum. During the drive we talked ourselves into a belated enthusiasm for Army Co-operation, and as we came on to the road skirting the aerodrome and saw the field slanting downhill from the hangars with machines picketed around the edge, we gazed at them with interest. There were an equal number of Hectors and Lysanders, heroic enough names though the machines might belie them in appearance. The Hectors were slim biplanes, advanced editions of the old Hart, but it was the Lysanders, the machines in which it seemed probable that we should be flying for the duration, that really caught our attention. They were squat, heavy, high-winged monoplanes and looked as though they could take a beating. We were less impressed by the two solitary guns, one fixed and firing forward and the other rotatable by the rear gunner.

The road running up to the Mess took us close by Salisbury, and the towering steeple of its cathedral was a good landmark from the aerodrome. The countryside lay quiet in the warm glow of the summer evening. A few minutes' flying to the south was the sea, and across from it France, equally peaceful in the quiet of the evening; within a few weeks Britain's army was to be struggling desperately to get back across that narrow stretch of water, and the France that we knew was to be no more.

The Course was run with great efficiency by a dapper little Squadron Leader by the name of Barker. We were divided into squads and spent from nine o'clock in the morning to seven in the evening alternating between lectures and flying our two types of aircraft.

To our delight, on the second day of the Course Bill Aitken appeared from Cranwell to join us. We had not seen him since together with most of our friends he had been posted to his F.T.S. several months before. He was the same as ever, rather serious, with deep lines across his broad forehead and little bursts of dry laughter. He did his best to answer all our questions, but when we got around to Frank Waldron and Nigel Bicknell he was inclined to become a little pompous. It appeared that the regulations at Cranwell had been somewhat more strictly enforced than in Scotland. Frank and Nigel had set off with much the same ideas as Noel and I up in Scotland, but with more determination as the rules were stricter, and consequently they had come up against more trouble.

They had consistently attempted to avoid lectures, and Frank had crowned his efforts by oversleeping for the Wings Exam. He was also violently sick whenever he went up (which was not his fault), so the Air Ministry raised little objection when he applied for a transfer to the Scots Guards.

Nigel, it appeared, had found the restrictions an irresistible attraction, and no notice could appear without him hearing of it; he would solemnly produce pieces of red tape from his pocket and pin them around the board. This did not tend to encourage cordial relations with the higher authorities, and when he finally wrote an extremely witty but hardly tactful letter to the Commanding Officer, pointing out that Volunteer Reservists had joined the R.A.F. to fight the Germans and not to be treated like children, his stock was at its lowest ebb. He was not actually kicked out, but his record sheet was the blackest of the Course and his action resulted in a tightening-up of all restrictions.

" When I left Cranwell," said Bill, " he was trying to hook himself a job as Air Force Psychologist."

It was obvious that Bill did not approve, and one could not blame him. He thought their actions represented something deeper than mere fooling-about, a disinclination to face up to the war and a desire to avoid fighting it for as long as possible. He thought further that there were a dangerous number of young men with pseudo-intellectual leanings in the same direction — this last with a significant glance at me.

I disagreed with him. I thought he had made a superficial assessment and said so. I went further : I prophesied that within six months he would have to take those words back, that those very people who were being so unstable at the moment would prove themselves as capable as anyone of facing an emergency when the time came. "I doubt it," he said. "Anyway you know that war has been described as 'a period of great boredom, interspersed with moments of great excitement.' The man who believes enough in what he's fighting for to put up with the periods of boredom is twice as important in the winning of a war as the man who rises to a crisis."

Besides Bill we discovered two other familiar figures, Peter Pease and Colin Pinckney. They had both been in the Cambridge Air Squadron before the war. Peter was, I think, the best-looking man I have ever seen. He stood six-foot-three and was of a deceptive slightness for he weighed close on 13 stone. He had an outward reserve which protected him from any surface friendships, but for those who troubled to get to know him it was apparent that this reserve masked a deep shyness and a profound integrity of character. Soft-spoken, and with an innate habit of understatement, I never knew him to lose his temper. He never spoke of himself, and it was only through Colin that I learned how well he had done at Eton before his two reflective years at Cambridge, where he had watched events in Europe and made up his mind what part he must play when the exponents of everything he most abhorred began to sweep all before them.

Colin was of the same height but of broader build. He had a bony, pleasantly ugly face and openly admitted that he derived most of his pleasure in life from a good grouse-shoot and a well-proportioned salmon. He was somewhat more forthcoming than Peter but of fundamentally the same instincts. They had been together since the beginning of the war and were now inseparable. I was to become the third corner of a triangle of friendship the record of which will form an important part of the rest of this book. It is therefore perhaps well to stress that Peter Pease, and not Peter Howes, is the peak of this triangle.

The work at Old Sarum was interesting. We studied detailed-map reading, aerial photography, air-to-ground Morse, artillery shoots, and long-distance reconnaissance. The Lysander proved to be a ponderous old gentleman's plane, heavy on the controls but easy to handle. It seemed almost impossible to stall it.

Of flying incidents there were few, though once I did my best to kill my observer. We were on our way back from a photography sortie when I decided to do some aerobatics. As our Inter-Comm. was not working, I turned round, pointed at the observer, and then tapped my straps, to ask him if he was adequately tied in. He nodded. I started off by doing a couple of stall turns. Behind me I could hear him shouting away in what I took to be an involuntary access of enthusiastic approval. After the second stall turn I put the machine into a loop. On the dive down he leaned forward and shouted in my ear. I waved my hand. On the climb up, I saw him out of the corner of my eye letting himself low down into the rear seat. Then we were up and over. I straightened up and looked back. There was no sign of my observer. I shouted. Still he did not appear. I had a sudden feeling of apprehension. That shouting — could it mean . . . ? I peered anxiously over the side. At that moment a white face emerged slowly from the back cockpit, a hand grabbed my shoulder and a voice shouted in my ear : " For Christ's sake don't do a slow roll, I'm not strapped in ! "

He had taken my signals for a query whether I was strapped in. His cries had been not of joy but of fear, and when we had started down on our loop he had dived rapidly to the bottom of the cockpit, clutching feverishly at the camera on the floor for support and convinced that his last hour had come.

I headed back for the aerodrome and, after making a quick circuit, deposited him gingerly on the field, landing as though I had dynamite in the back.

Noel nearly cut short a promising flying career in a Hector. He opened up to take off with the pasteboard instructions for his second Morse exercise on his knee. As the machine gathered speed across the aerodrome the card had dropped from his knee on to the floor. He bent to pick it up, inadvertently pushing the stick further forward as he did so. The long prop touched the ground and the machine tore its nose in and somersaulted on to its back. It did not catch fire. As the ambulance shot out from the hangars, I remember muttering to myself: "Pray God don't be a bloody fool and undo the straps." Fortunately he did not and escaped with a badly cut tongue and a warning from the C.F.I. that a repetition of the episode would not be treated lightly.

A surprising number of people have managed to kill themselves by putting on their brakes too hard when coming in to land, toppling on to their backs, and then undoing the straps — to fall out on their heads and break their necks.

Every night at nine o'clock the Mess was crowded with Army and Air Force officers, men who commonly never bothered to listen to the news, parked round the radio with silent expressionless faces, listening to the extermination of France and the desperate retreat of the British Expeditionary Force.

Privately we learned that Lysanders were hopping across the Channel two or three times daily in an effort to drop supplies to the besieged garrison in Calais, sometimes with a solitary one-gunned Hector for fighter support. As the Lysander was supposed to operate always under a covering layer of fighters, we could imagine how desperate the situation must be.

Then came Dunkirk : tired, ragged men who had once been an army, returning now with German souvenirs but without their own equipment ; and the tendency of the public to regard it almost as a victory.

After days on the beaches without sight of British planes these men were bitter, and not unnaturally. They could not be expected to know that, had we not for once managed to gain air superiority behind them, over Flanders, they would never have left Dunkirk alive. For us the evacuation was still a newspaper story, until Noel, Howes, and I got the day off, motored to Brighton, and saw for ourselves.

The beaches, streets, and pubs were a crawling mass of soldiers, British, French, and Belgian. They had no money but were being royally welcomed by the locals. They were ragged and weary. When Howes suddenly met a blonde and vanished with her and the car for the rest of the day, Noel and I soon found ourselves in various billets acting as interpreters for the French. They were very tired and very patient. It had been so long. What could a few more hours matter ? The most frequent request was for somewhere to bathe their feet. When it became obvious that there had been a mix-up, that some billets looked like being hopelessly overcrowded and others empty, we gave up. Collecting two French soldiers and a Belgian dispatch rider, we took them off for a drink. The bar we chose was a seething mass of sweating, turbulent khaki. Before we could even get a drink we were involved in half a dozen arguments over the whereabouts of our aircraft over Dunkirk. Knowing personally several pilots who had been killed, and with some knowledge of the true facts, we found it hard to keep our tempers.

In fairness to the B.E.F. it must be said that by no means all returned as rabble. A story of the Grenadier Guards was already going the rounds. In columns of three they had marched on to the pier at Dunkirk with complete equipment, as though going for a route march. A Territorial officer, seeing them standing at ease, advanced and started to distribute spoons and forks for them to deal with the food that was being handed out. His efforts were summarily halted by the acid comment of a young Grenadier subaltern :

" Thank you," he said, " but the Grenadiers always carry their own cutlery."

The French were less bitter, possibly out of politeness, but more probably because while they had seen few British aircraft, they had seen no French. But it was our Belgian dispatch rider who surprised and delighted us by endorsing everything we said.

" How could we expect to see many British Fighter planes ? " he asked. " There was a heavy fog over the beaches and they were up above."

One fight, however, he had seen — a lone Spitfire among four Junkers. For him, he said, it had been symbolic, and he admitted having prayed. If that Spitfire came out on top, then they would all be rescued. His prayer was answered. It shot down two Germans, crippled a third, and the fourth made off.

We sat on till well into the night, talking, arguing, singing, getting tight ; they, tired and relaxed, content to sit back, their troubles for the moment over, we taut and expectant, braced by our first real contact with the war, eager to get started.

Finally, through an alcoholic haze, we made our farewells and staggered out into the street. Somehow we located both Howes and the car and set off back for Old Sarum. We were late and Howes drove fast. There was no moon. Coming out of a bend, he took the bank with his near-side front wheel, skidded, touched the brake, and hit the bank again. We were still travelling fast. For a moment we hung on two wheels, and then we turned over, once, twice. There was a crash of splintering glass, a tearing noise as two of the doors were torn off, and then, but for the sound of escaping petrol, silence. That week I had bought myself a new service cap and I could see it wedged under Noel's left knee.

"Get off my cap, blast you!" I shouted, thus destroying the silence and bringing down on my head a storm of invective, from which I gathered that none of us was seriously hurt. It turned out that we hadn't even a scratch. "It looks," said Howes, " as though Fate doesn't want us to go out this way. Maybe we have a more exciting death in store for us." Looking back, unpleasantly prophetic words.

A day or so later all leave was cancelled, no one was allowed further than half an hour's call from the aerodrome, and the invasion scare was on. An order came that all officers were to carry side arms, and at the station armoury I was issued with an antiquated short-nosed Forty-five and six soft-lead bullets. I appealed to the armament sergeant.

"Sorry, sir," he said, "but that's the regulation. Just content yourself with six Jerries, sir."

That in itself would not have been so bad if only the ammunition fitted, which I soon found it did not. With only six bullets there was little temptation to waste any of them practising, but one day by low cunning I managed to get myself another twelve and loosed off. The first round fired but the second jammed. I had .455 bullets for a .45 revolver.

The Government's appeal to the people to stay put and not to evacuate, printed on the front page of every newspaper, roused England to the imminence of disaster. It could actually happen. England's green and pleasant land might at any moment wake to the noise of thundering tanks, to the sight of an army dropping from the skies, and to the realization that it was too late.

In Government departments, city offices, and warehouses, in farms, schools, and universities, the civilian population of England woke up. It was their war. From seventeen to seventy they came forward for the Home Guard. If they had no arms — and usually they hadn't — they drilled with brooms. The spirit was there, but the arms and the organization were not.

At Old Sarum we had completed our six weeks and were ready for drafting to our Squadrons. Then the inevitable happened, though at that time it seemed more like a miracle. It started as a rumour, but when the whole Course was called together and the chief instructor rose to his feet, rumour became reality.

Owing to the sudden collapse of France and our own consequent vulnerability it had been decided that a number of us were to go to Fighter Squadrons. The Air Ministry had ordered fifteen to be transferred. We each looked at our neighbour as though he were suddenly an enemy. There were twenty of us, and the five who were to continue in Army Co-operation were to be drawn from a hat. It was my worst moment of the war, and I speak for all the others.

Bill Aitken and Peter Pease were both drawn, together with three others. The rest of us almost groaned with relief. But it seemed hard on Peter, though he made no complaint. It would mean his separation from Colin and the loss of a potentially great fighter pilot.

For Bill it did not matter : he was older, that type of flying appealed to him, and he was admirably suited for it. I think he was not too disappointed. The fighter pilots were to go to an Operational Training Unit in Gloucestershire close to the Welsh border, for a fortnight. Then our training would be complete and we would be drafted to Fighter Squadrons.

Of us all, I think Noel was the most elated. His face wore a permanent fixed grin which nothing could wipe off.

" Spitfires at last," he kept repeating.

" Spitfires or Hurricanes," I said meanly.

He continued to grin.

" Don't give a damn. They're both good enough for me."

We were to leave at once. At the last moment one other man was required and Peter Pease was selected ; so it was in a contented frame of mind that we set off.

To our delight our instructors were No. 1 Squadron, back from France and being given a rest. There is little need for me to say much about them, for through Noel Monk's account in *Squadrons Up* of the part they played at Maastricht Bridge and elsewhere at the front, they must be about the best-known Squadron in the R.A.F.

"Bull" Halahan was still their Commanding Officer, and Johnnie Walker was in charge of flying. They were the first decorated pilots of this war that we had seen and we regarded them with considerable awe. They were not unaware of this and affected a pointed nonchalance. The Bull was so much what one had expected as to be almost a caricature. A muscled stocky figure with a prominent jaw and an Irish twinkle in his eye, he would roll into the lecture room and start right in with whatever he had to say.

These men treated us as junior members of a Squadron. They were friendly and casual, but they expected cooperation and they got it. It was a pleasant change from Training Command. Time was short and we had much to learn.

We learned many things then new, though perhaps no longer true, so swiftly do fighter tactics change. We learned for the first time the German habit of using their fighter escorts in stepped-up layers all around their bombers, their admitted excellence in carrying out some prearranged manœuvre, and their confusion and ineffectiveness once this was in any way disturbed.

We learned of the advantage of height and of attacking from out of the sun; of the Germans' willingness to fight with height and odds in their favour and their disinclination to mix it on less favourable terms; of the vulnerability of the Messerschmitt

109 when attacked from the rear and its almost standardized method of evasion when so attacked — a half roll, followed by a vertical dive right down to the ground. As the Messerschmitt pilots had to sit on their petrol tanks, it is perhaps hard to blame them.

We learned of the necessity to work as a Squadron and to understand thoroughly every command of the Squadron Leader whether given by mouth or gesture.

We learned that we should never follow a plane down after hitting it, for it weakened the effectiveness of the Squadron ; and further was likely to result in an attack from the rear. This point was driven home by the example of five planes over Dunkirk all of which followed each other down. Only the top machine survived.

If we were so outnumbered that we were forced to break formation, we should attempt to keep in pairs, and never for more than two seconds fly on a straight course. In that moment we might forget all we had ever learned about Rate-1 turns and keeping a watchful eye on the turn-and-bank indicator. We should straighten up only when about to attack, closing in to 200 yards, holding the machine steady in the turbulent slipstream of the other plane, and letting go with all eight guns in short snap bursts of from two to four seconds.

We learned of the German mass psychology applied even to their planes, of how they were so constructed that the crews were always bunched together, thus gaining confidence and a false sense of security.

We learned the importance of getting to know our ground crews and to appreciate their part in a successful day's fighting, to make a careful check-up before taking off, but not to be hypercritical, for the crews would detect and resent any lack of confidence at once.

And we learned, finally, to fly the Spitfire.

I faced the prospect with some trepidation. Here for the first time was a machine in which there was no chance of making a dual circuit as a preliminary. I must solo right off, and in the fastest machine in the world.

One of the Squadron took me up for a couple of trips in a Miles Master, the British trainer most similar to a Spitfire in characteristics.

I was put through half an hour's instrument flying under the hood in a Harvard, and then I was ready. At least I hoped I was ready. Kilmartin, a slight dark-haired Irishman in charge of our Flight, said : " Get your parachute and climb in. I'll just show you the cockpit before you go off."

He sauntered over to the machine, and I found myself memorizing every detail of his appearance with the clearness of a condemned man on his way to the scaffold — the chin sunk into the folds of a polo sweater, the leather pads on the elbows, and the string-darned hole in the seat of the pants. He caught my look of anxiety and grinned.

" Don't worry ; you'll be surprised how easy she is to handle."

I hoped so.

The Spitfires stood in two lines outside " A " Flight Pilots' room. The dull grey-brown of the camouflage could not conceal the clear-cut beauty, the wicked simplicity of their lines. I hooked up my parachute and climbed awkwardly into the low cockpit. I noticed how small was my field of vision. Kilmartin swung himself on to a wing and started to run through the instruments. I was conscious of his voice, but heard nothing of what he said. I was to fly a Spitfire. It was what I had most wanted through all the long dreary months of training. If I could fly a Spitfire, it would be worth it. Well, I was about to achieve my ambition and felt nothing. I was numb, neither exhilarated nor scared. I noticed the white enamel undercarriage handle. " Like a lavatory plug," I thought.

" What did you say ? "

Kilmartin was looking at me and I realized I had spoken aloud. I pulled myself together.

" Have you got all that ? " he asked.

" Yes, sir."

" Well, off you go then. About four circuits and bumps. Good luck ! "

He climbed down.

I taxied slowly across the field, remembering suddenly what I had been told : that the Spitfire's prop was long and that it was therefore inadvisable to push the stick too far forward when taking off; that the Spitfire was not a Lysander and that any hard application of the brake when landing would result in a somersault and immediate transfer to a "Battle" Squadron. Because of the Battle's lack of power and small armament this was regarded by everyone as the ultimate disgrace.

I ran quickly through my cockpit drill, swung the nose into wind, and took off. I had been flying automatically for several minutes before it dawned on me that I was actually in the air, undercarriage retracted and half-way round the circuit without incident. I turned into wind and hauled up on my seat, at the same time pushing back the hood. I came in low, cut the engine just over the boundary hedge, and floated down on all three points. I took off again. Three more times I came round for a perfect landing. It was too easy. I waited across wind for a minute and watched with satisfaction several machines bounce badly as they came in. Then I taxied rapidly back to the hangars and climbed out nonchalantly. Noel, who had not yet soloed, met me.

" How was it ? " he said.

I made a circle of approval with my thumb and forefinger.

" Money for old rope," I said.

I didn't make another good landing for a week.

The flight immediately following our first solo was an hour's aerobatics. I climbed up to 12,000 feet before attempting even a slow roll.

Kilmartin had said " See if you can make her talk." That meant the whole bag of tricks, and I wanted ample room for mistakes and possible blacking-out. With one or two very sharp movements on the stick I blacked myself out for a few seconds, but the machine was sweeter to handle than any other that I had flown. I put it through every manœuvre that I knew of and it responded beautifully. I ended with two flick rolls and turned back for home. I was filled with a sudden exhilarating confidence. I could fly a Spitfire ; in any position I was its master. It remained to be seen whether I could fight in one.

We also had to put in an oxygen climb to 28,000 feet, an air-firing exercise, formation attacks, and numerous dog-fights.

The oxygen climb was uneventful but lengthy. It was interesting to see what a distance one ended up from the aerodrome even though climbing all the way in wide circles. Helmet, goggles, and oxygen mask gave me a feeling of restriction, and from then on I always flew with my goggles up, except when landing. The results of this were to be far-reaching.

The air-firing exercise was uneventful, but as short

as the oxygen climb had been long. We were given
a few rounds in each gun and sent off to fire them
into the Severn. All eight guns roared out from a
quick pressure on the fire button on the control stick.
The noise through the enclosed cabin was muffled,
but the recoil caused a momentary drop in speed of
40 miles per hour.

For our formation attack practices we usually
needed six machines. We flew in two sections of
three with an instructor heading each. One section
would fly along in V formation representing the
enemy and the other would make an attack. The
attacking section would also fly in V formation until
the enemy were sighted. Then the section leader
would call out over the radio telephone " Line
astern ! " and the pilots to right and left of him would
drop behind.

A section in line astern is in its most manœuvrable
formation. The leader would then come up on the
enemy formation, taking care to keep well out to
one side (usually to starboard) and a few hundred
feet above them. When still some distance off, he
would call out " Echelon starboard ! " and the two
following machines would draw out to his right, still
keeping fairly tight formation. When about 300
yards astern and to starboard of the enemy, he would
call out " Going down ! " and all three machines, still
in echelon formation, would dive down and come up

behind the target aircraft. At about 250 yards' range
they would open fire (theoretically), and close in more
slowly to about 100 yards when the leader would call
out "Breaking away!" and with an abrupt movement of stick and rudder go tearing downwards and
sideways beneath the enemy machines, thus giving the
rear gunners, if they were still alive, a double factor
to allow for when taking their aim. The other two
machines would follow and form up again in line
astern, this time to port of the enemy and in a position
to repeat the attack. We came up in echelon to avoid
cross fire — assuming the target aircraft to be bombers
— and we broke away downwards to avoid presenting
the bellies of our machines to the rear gunners. If the
target aircraft were fighters, we broke away upwards,
as they had no rear gunners, and by doing so we at
the same time gained height.

When we were sent up for a dog-fight, two of us
would go off together for forty minutes and endea-
vour in every way possible to "shoot" each other
down. One learned most from this exercise, of
course, when an instructor was in the other plane ;
but there were many pilots and few instructors, so
this was a rarity. On one occasion I went up with
Kilmartin. We climbed to 10,000 feet, and he inti-
mated that he would attempt to get on my tail. He
succeeded. In frenzied eagerness I hurled my machine
about the sky. Never, I felt, had such things been

done to a plane. They must inevitably dislodge him. But a quick glance in my mirror showed that he was quietly behind me like a patient nursemaid following a too boisterous charge. Only once did I nearly succeed. I did a particularly tight turn and inadvertently went into a spin which took me into a cloud. For a moment I had lost him, but I had lost myself too, and thus restored the *status quo*.

When we re-established contact, he signalled to me to get on his tail and stay there. I carried out the first part of my orders admirably and started to pursue him round in ever-tightening circles. I attempted to get him in my sights, but could not quite succeed in doing so. But that did not prevent me from wondering why he calmly allowed me to follow him without taking any evasive action : these circles were becoming monotonous and making me dizzy. I glanced in my mirror and understood. I was dead long ago, and I could almost imagine that I saw him smile. I was very glad it was a practice.

I landed considerably mortified and prepared for some withering comments. Kilmartin climbed out of his machine with a sly grin at the corner of his mouth.

" Do you feel as dead as you should ? " he asked.

I nodded.

" That's all right," he said. " I meant you to. Now I'll give you a few tips for the next time."

He told me then of the uselessness of all aerobatics

in actual combat. Their only value was to give a pilot a feeling of mastery over his machine in any position, upright or inverted. To do a loop was to present a slow-moving sitting target to your opponent, who need only raise the nose of his machine slightly to keep you permanently in his sights. A slow roll was little better. For complete evasion the two most effective methods were a half roll and a controlled spin — especially if you had been hit, for it gave an impression of being out of control. For the rest it was a question of turning inside your opponent (sometimes pulling up and above him, the more effectively to dive down again), of thinking quickly and clearly, of seizing every opportunity and firing at once, and of a quick break-away. All this and more he impressed upon me, and I did my best to carry it out on my subsequent flights. These were less one-sided, but then I never flew with him again.

On these dog-fights we would also practise beam attacks, probably the most effective and certainly the most difficult means of bringing down an enemy machine. The attacking Spitfire would overhaul his target, well out to the side and about 500 feet or so above. When some little way ahead he would bank and turn in, to let the other machine come through his sights almost at right angles, and with a double deflection (twice the diameter of his sights) he would let go in a long burst. He thus opened fire in front of the enemy's nose and raked him all the way down the side where he had the least protection and the smallest field of fire, while himself presenting a very small and awkwardly moving target for the gunners. He could then drop in behind and deliver another attack from the rear.

But my clearest memory of the course was the bridge. It was across the Severn and linked England to Wales. It was a narrow bridge with close-set arches and it was the occasion of a long-brewing quarrel for Noel and me.

Noel, Peter Howes, and I had been together now for some time and were beginning to get on one another's nerves. There was soon to be a parting of the ways. It happened at the very end of our training, when we were about to join our Squadrons, and was to have consequences which none of us could foresee, which all three of us vaguely sensed, but yet could do nothing to stop. With Howes it took the form of withdrawing into himself, of saying little and of avoiding our company. For Noel and me, fundamentally closer together and considerably quicker-tempered, it could not end like that. There had to be a show-down : the bridge provided it.

Noel, low-flying down the Severn, came to the bridge and flew under it. He came back and told me. From then on the bridge fascinated and frightened me. I had to fly under it. I said as much to Peter Pease.

He gave me a long quizzical stare.

"Richard," he said, "from now on a lot of people are going to fly under that bridge. From a flying point of view it proves nothing : it's extremely stupid. From a personal point of view it can only be of value if you don't tell anybody about it."

He was right of course.

To fly under the bridge now simply to come back and say that I had done so would be sheer exhibitionism. It would prove nothing. Yet I knew I would fly under it. I had to for my own satisfaction, just as many years before I had had to stand on a 25-foot board above a swimming-pool until I dived off.

There was a strongish wind blowing, and as I came down to a few feet above the river I saw that I had on quite an amount of drift. The span of the arch looked depressingly narrow ; I considered pulling up but forced myself to hold the stick steady. For a moment I thought I was going to hit with the port wing, and then I was through.

It was later in the Mess and we were playing billiards when Noel asked me if I had done it. By now we could not even play billiards without the game developing into a silently bitter struggle for supremacy. As Noel nearly always won, he could not have chosen a worse moment to speak.

"Well, did you ?" he asked.

I played a deliberate shot and didn't answer.

He laughed.

"Surely our little winged wonder isn't getting soft? I was expecting to hear how narrowly you missed death."

I put down my cue.

"Listen, Noel," I said. "For months you've been smugly satisfied that you're a better pilot than I am, and just because I soloed before you here you have to go off and make a bloody fool of yourself under some bridge just to prove that you're still a hell of a pilot. You make me sick."

He looked at me bitterly.

"Well, little Lord Fauntleroy, this *is* a new angle. And from you, the biggest line-shooter I've ever known. All right. Stick around the hangars cadging extra flights and crawling to the instructors. Maybe they'll give you a good assessment yet." And with that he slammed red into a corner pocket to win the game and I stalked out of the room and slammed the door.

Next day Squadron vacancies were announced. I walked down to the Adjutant's office with Peter Pease and Colin Pinckney. 603 (City of Edinburgh) Squadron had three vacancies. It was out of the battle area (the first battle over Dover had already been fought), but it was a Spitfire Squadron and we could all three go together. We put our names down. Noel decided to go to Northolt to 609 Squadron to fly Hurricanes, and Peter Howes to Hornchurch to 54 Squadron.

The following day we left. I was to drive up with Peter Pease and we were to make an early start. I piled my luggage into his car and prepared to climb in after it. Then I hesitated and turned back. I found Noel packing. He got up as I came in. We were both embarrassed. I held out my hand.

"Good-bye and good luck," I said.

"Good-bye, Dick," he said. "We've drifted rather a long way apart lately. I'm sorry. Don't let's either of us drift up to Heaven. That's all."

While he was speaking Peter Howes had come in to say good-bye too. "You two needn't worry," he said. "You both have the luck of the devil. If the long-haired boys are to be broken up, I have a hunch that I'll be the first to go." We both told him not to be a fool and agreed to meet, all three of us, in three months' time in London.

They came out to the car.

"Take care of yourself," said Peter Howes.

"Your courage amazes me," said Noel. "Going back to that bloody awful country, and voluntarily !"

I waved and then Peter Pease and I were round the corner and on our way. I sat silent most of the way to London, confused by a number of disturbing emotions.

# 4
## The World of Peter Pease

WE had two days in which to get to Edinburgh and we spent one night in London, a London still unscarred and carefree, before driving up to Yorkshire, where we intended to break our journey at the Peases'.

Peter drove fast and well, without any of the sudden bursts of acceleration which characterize most fast drivers. For some reason I was surprised. Upright in his seat, his existence was concentrated in his hands on the wheel and in the sole of his foot on the accelerator. There was little traffic on the roads and as we moved out into the open country all nature seemed to sing with the rhythm of the tyres on the hot asphalt. Gradually the countryside turned from a soft green warmth to a gaunt bleakness. I was a little depressed, for we had heard a rumour that Scottish Squadrons would not cross the Border. To kick our heels in Scotland with the war at last about to break in the South was not my idea of a design for living. Peter was unruffled and satisfied that we should be in the thick of it before many weeks were past, but with every mile my depression deepened.

"God, how I hate the North," I said, "the country, the climate, the people; all craggy, dour, and shut-in. I can go south to France, Italy, or where you will and feel perfectly at home; but north of Oxford I'm in a foreign country."

Peter laughed. "That's because at heart you're a man of the capital. You live in London, and you understand it and like it and like the people; but you get up to Manchester or Birmingham, and you see their ugliness with unprejudiced eyes. It appals you. I don't blame you, it appals me too; but then so does ugliness in London. I'm not prejudiced in London's favour, as you are."

"Oh, no, it's not only the towns, it's the country too. What could you have more beautiful than Buckinghamshire — or if it's not beautiful, it's warm and attractive, which is much more important. But as for this——" I waved my hand vaguely out of the window, where the Black Country stretched out wet and dreary on either side.

Peter nodded. "Yes, it looks pretty ghastly, doesn't it? Yet it all fits in. The people who live here love the grime and the stench and the living conditions. They've never known anything else and it's a part of them. That's why they'll fight this war to the end rather than surrender one inch of it."

I thought for a moment I was going to get him into an argument about the war, but as soon as he saw what I was after he steered the conversation politely away and it was not for another six weeks that I was to break down his silence.

We arrived in time for dinner, and the crunch of the tyres on the drive as we swung through the gates prepared me for the comfortably substantial house in front of which we drew up. Colin Pinckney arrived half an hour later, having driven up in a more leisurely manner, and we went in to dinner. The Peases were a devoted family and Peter's parents quite obviously adored him. In that quiet dining-room with just the five of us gathered round the table it occurred to me that if Peter were killed, it would be important — not only to his family, but indeed for me, as the deaths of the majority of my friends many of whom I knew better could not be. I was confused and disturbed by this.

After dinner Lady Pease was discussing an offer she had had to send one of her boys, now at Eton, to America, an offer which she had turned down. She felt that it was a bad precedent for well-to-do children to be sent abroad and a very bad preparation for life in a post-war England. I agreed with her. I thought of the surprising number of men in responsible positions who seemed determined to get their wives and children out of the country. I didn't quite understand it. The natural reason would be that they didn't want them hurt, but I wasn't sure that that was the whole of it. I didn't believe that a man with something important to do in this war wanted the responsibility of a wife, more especially if he loved her. She was a distracting liability and he would be far happier with her out of the way. Then he could concentrate his whole mind on his job without having to wonder the whole time whether she was safe. All he needed was the purely physical satisfaction of some woman, and that he could get anywhere.

Now, at the Peases', on the way to bed, I asked Colin if he thought that were true. "To a certain extent," he replied, " but like all your generalizations it doesn't by any means apply universally. For example, how do you fit in all these hurried war marriages with your theory ? "

"I admit they don't seem to fit into the picture at first, but I think we can explain them. I don't know if you've noticed it, and again this is one of my generalizations, but it's been almost entirely the little men who have got married."

"What do you mean," he asked, " the little men ? "

"Well, as far as I can see, in the Army, and certainly in all Squadrons, it's been the nonentity, the fellow who was unsure of himself, standing drinks, always laughing and singing songs in the Mess, trying to be one of the chaps and never quite succeeding.

He doesn't feel himself accepted by the others and somehow he's got to prove himself, so he does it by marrying some poor, clinging little girl, giving her a child to justify his manhood and then getting killed. She's left with £90 a year, and I hope, a pleasant memory."

But Colin, muttering about cynics and how late it was, was already on his way to bed.

Early next morning we were on our way. It was cold in Edinburgh and the damp mist lay heavy on the streets. We drove straight out to the aerodrome at Turnhouse and reported to our C.O., Squadron Leader Denholm (known by the Squadron as Uncle George). From him we learned that the Squadron was operating further north, "A" Flight from Dyce and "B" Flight from Montrose. There was one Spitfire replacement to be flown up to Dyce; Colin got the job and so it came about that Peter and I drove up together to join "B" Flight at Montrose.

The aerodrome lay just beyond the town and stretched parallel to the sea, one edge of the landing field merging into the dunes. For a few miles around the country was flat, but mountain peaks reared abruptly into the sky, forming a purple backdrop for the aerodrome.

The first person to greet us in the Mess was Michael Judd, whom neither of us had seen since our initial training. He was an instructor. He took us down to the Dispersal Point to introduce us to the Squadron. Montrose was primarily an F.T.S. where future pilots crowded the air in Miles Masters. As the only possible enemy raids must come from Norway, half a Squadron was considered sufficient for its protection.

At our Dispersal Point at the north-west corner of the aerodrome there were three wooden huts. One of these was the Flight Commander's office; another was reserved for the R.T. equipment and technicians; the third, divided into two, was for the pilots and ground crew respectively. It was into this third hut that Michael led us.

From the ceiling hung several models of German aircraft, on the back wall by the stove were pasted seductive creatures by Petty, and on a table in the middle of the room a gramophone was playing, propped at a drunken angle on a pile of old books and magazines. In a corner there was another table on which there were a couple of telephones operated by a corporal. Two beds standing against the longer walls, and several old chairs, completed the furniture.

As we came in, half a dozen heads were turned towards the door and Rushmer, the Flight Commander, came forward to greet us. Like the others, he wore a Mae West and no tunic. Known by everyone as Rusty on account of his dull-red hair, he had a shy manner and a friendly smile. Peter, I could see, sensed a kindred spirit at once. Rusty never ordered things to be done ; he merely suggested that it might be a good idea if they were done, and they always were. He had a bland manner and an ability tacitly to ignore anything which he did not wish to hear, which protected him alike from outside interference from his superiors and from too frequent suggestions from his junior officers on how to run the Flight. Rusty had been with the Squadron since before the war : he was a Flight Lieutenant, and in action always led the Red Section. As 603 was an Auxiliary Squadron, all the older members were people with civilian occupations who before the war had flown for pleasure.

Blue Section Leader Larry Cunningham had also been with the Squadron for some time. He was a Scotsman, tall and thin, without Rusty's charm, but with plenty of experience.

Then there was Brian Carbury, a New Zealander who had started in 41 Squadron. He was six-foot-four, with crinkly hair and a roving eye. He greeted us warmly and suggested an immediate adjournment to the Mess for drinks. Before the war he had been a shoe salesman in New Zealand. Sick of the job, he had come to England and taken a short service commission. He was now a Flying Officer. There was little distinctive about him on the ground, but he was to prove the Squadron's greatest asset in the air.

Another from overseas was Hugh Stapleton, a
South African. He hoped to return after the war and
run an orange farm. He too was over six feet tall,
thick-set, with a mass of blond hair which he never
brushed. He was twenty and married, with a rough
*savoir-faire* beyond his years, acquired from an early
unprotected acquaintance with life. He was always
losing buttons off his uniform and had a pair of
patched trousers which the rest of the Squadron swore
he slept in. He was completely slap-happy and known
as " Stapme " because of his predilection for Popeye
in the *Daily Mirror*, his favourite literature.

Pilot Officer Berry, commonly known as Raspberry, came from Hull. He was short and stocky,
with a ruddy complexion and a mouth that was
always grinning or coming out with some broad
Yorkshire witticism impossible to answer. Above
that mouth, surprisingly, sprouted a heavy black
moustache, which induced me to call him the organ-
grinder. His reply to this was always unprintable but
very much to the point. Even on the blackest days
he radiated an infectious good-humour. His aggressive spirit chafed at the Squadron's present inactivity
and he was always the first to hear any rumour of our
moving south.

" Bubble " Waterston was twenty-four, but he
looked eighteen, with his short-cropped hair and open
face. He too had been with the Squadron for some

time before the war. He had been studying in Scotland for an engineering degree. He had great curiosity about anything mechanical, and was always tinkering with the engine of his car. His unquestioning acceptance of everyone and his unconscious charm made him the most popular member of the Squadron.

Then there was Boulter, with jutting ears framing the face of an intelligent ferret, always sleepy and in bed snoring when off duty; "Broody" Benson, nineteen years old, a fine pilot and possessed of only one idea, to shoot down Huns, more Huns, and then still more Huns; Don MacDonald who had been in the Cambridge Squadron and had an elder brother in " A " Flight at Dyce; and finally Pip Cardell, the most recent addition to the Squadron before our arrival, still bewildered, excited, and a little lost.

For the first week or so, Peter and I were not to be operational. We would have a chance to utilize the Squadron's comparative inactivity to acquaint ourselves thoroughly with the flying idiosyncrasies of the others.

All that we had on duty at a time was one Readiness Section of three machines: the rest of the Squadron were either available (ready to take off within half an hour of a call) or released (allowed off the aerodrome). With a full complement of pilots, it was nearly always possible for two of us to get up into the hills for a couple of days a week, where we shot grouse. The same system applied to " A " Flight at Dyce.

At this time the Germans were sending over single raiders from Norway, and with six Spitfires between Dyce and Montrose there was little difficulty in shooting them down. Operations would ring through, the corporal at the telephone in the pilots' room would call out, " Red Section scramble base," one of us would fire a red Very light to clear the air of all training aircraft, and within a couple of minutes three machines would be in the air climbing rapidly. The leader, in constant radio touch with the ground, would be given a course on which to fly to intercept the enemy. So good was the ground control that it was not infrequent to make an interception forty miles out to sea. The Section would then carry out a copybook attack ; the bomber would come down in the sea, and her crew, if still alive, would push off in a rubber boat, waving frantically. The Section would radio back the derelicts' position, turn for home, and that would be that.

On one occasion, when I was still not operational, I was flying up the coast when I heard Operations order our Blue Section into the air and start radioing the bomber's position. I should have returned to the base ; but instead I grabbed my map and pin-pointed its position — about four miles south of me and heading out to sea. Without reporting my intention, I set off after it, delighted at the prospect of returning and nonchalantly announcing its destruction single-handed.

It was a cloudy day and a fair guess that the enemy machine would be flying just in the bottom of the cloud base. Up to this minute I had behaved fairly rationally, but I now began a series of slow climbs and dives in and out of the clouds in search of my quarry. Finding nothing, I turned back and landed, to discover that two minutes earlier the enemy machine had flown right across the aerodrome at 1000 feet. It was not until Brian Carbury landed with his Section and inquired sweetly whether I'd had fun that I learned how nearly I had been killed. Having received no notice of any other friendly aircraft, and seeing a machine popping in and out of the clouds, he had put his Section into " line astern " and had been about to open fire when he recognized me as a Spitfire.

Next day Rusty made both Peter and me operational. " I think it will be safer for the others," he explained apologetically.

My first assignment, though not exciting, was for me particularly interesting. It meant flying down to Oxford. I had not been back since the war began and I was curious to see how different it would all seem now.

Noel had been there recently to see his family and had written to me : " Richard, whatever you do, don't go back. It would take a book to explain how it's changed; but to sum it up in one sentence — in the Randolph Bar there is a notice saying: 'No unaccompanied ladies will be served with drinks.'"

I flew down with one halt on the way and arrived in the early evening. I came down low and circled the city, looking for familiar landmarks. I picked out the Isis, a tiny mud-puddle, and the barges dotted along its bank; the Broad, and Trinity, with its well-kept gardens obvious from even that height; Longwall and Magdalen Tower. I made a couple of circuits and came in. This, the first part of my visit, was entirely satisfactory, for my bank manager was a member of the Home Guard and on duty at the time. He was suitably impressed with me as a pilot, and when next morning I called upon him, without much hope, for an extension of my overdraft, he was more than obliging.

On landing I called up Rusty and reported, then I hailed a taxi and drove straight down to Trinity.

Superficially it was unchanged. Huckins, the porter, was still at the gate. "Good evening, Mr. Hillary," he said, in the same lugubrious tone in which he would announce that one was to be reported to the Dean. The windows of my rooms over the chapel still looked out on the Quad and caught the evening rays of the sun, and a few old college servants raised friendly hands to their forelocks. But, apart from them, not a familiar face. It was of course out of term, but Trinity, unlike most colleges, had not been amalgamated or handed over to the Government, and I had hoped to see a few dons I knew. The old place was tired ; it had the left-over air of a seaside resort in winter. I walked into the garden quad and looked around at the uncurtained windows.

There was Algy Young's old room in which I had spent many an agreeable evening. Algy had looked like playing rugger for the University. Of a serious disposition, he could not make up his mind whether to go into politics or business. I remember how often we had laughed at him for his enjoyment of food and getting fat. Well, it was doubtful if he was enjoying either now in Oflag VII C, having been captured along with the rest of the Highland Division at Dunkirk.

And there was Staircase 15. Alwyn Stevens had had a room there. We had rowed together in the Head of the River Boat for two years. Moody and of uncertain temper as he was, the rest of us had not gone out of our way to understand him, and he had wrapped himself up in his work, surprising everyone when it was understood that he had a good chance of a First in Law. He had been killed flying.

Peter Krabbé had also been on that staircase. Boisterous, amusing, and sarcastic, he had not come back from France.

I climbed to my old room, intending to find

someone to make me up a bed for the night. All the furniture lay heaped in a corner, a mounted oar still hung over the fireplace, exaggerating if anything the bareness of the room. Geo. Coles had had the rooms before me. With his enormous shoulders he had been heavy-weight boxer for the University and a Rugger Blue. Of no enormous mental stature, he had not let it worry him and had led the life which amused him. At the beginning of the war he had managed to get a permanent commission in the Air Force : it was only a week since he had been seen going down in flames over France.

I kicked a chair-leg dispiritedly and went back down the stairs, intending to take a room for the night at the Randolph. I had no luggage. I hoped they'd try to stop me. At the bottom of the stairs I ran into the President's wife. She offered to put me up for the night. I accepted gratefully, explaining I might be late as I must go to the depot to make some arrangements. I then set off to survey the town. My first stop was the Randolph, where the truth of Noel's warning was forcibly brought home to me. The bar was full, but of strange faces, and Mary was no longer there to serve drinks. Some harassed creature pushed me a pink gin and forgot my change. I was about to give up and leave when I saw Eric Dehn. Eric and I had been to school together and we had done two years together at Oxford. He was in battle dress, and as amusing as ever. He had been in France but had got out at Dunkirk. He was as depressed as I, but we went along to the George for an excellent dinner and then on to the Playhouse to look up some of Eric's girl friends, with whom we passed a pleasant enough evening. It was very late when I got back to Trinity and took off my shoes, the more quietly to climb the President's stairs (one's education dies hard).

I was slightly drunk as I got undressed and crawled into bed. " This," I thought to myself hazily, " symbolizes everything. Tonight you sleep in the President's linen in your underpants ; tomorrow God knows ! " And with that I fell asleep. I was glad to go back to Montrose.

At this time we were still using Spitfires as night fighters. Now the Spitfire is not a good machine for night fighting. Its landing run is too long and the flames from its own exhaust make the pilot's visibility uncomfortably small. Shortly afterwards the whole problem of night interception was radically revised (with great success), but for the moment night fighting in Spitfires produced little more than hours to go in one's log-book. Three of us would spend the night in the Dispersal Hut waiting for a " flap." When it came, one machine would take off, and I as the junior squadron member would canter down the flare path, putting out all the lamps until the second machine

took off some ten minutes later, when I would put
them all on again. Meanwhile, there would be the
uneven hum of a German bomber circling above, an
experience which always gave me prickles down the
spine.

For the most part, life at Montrose was very agreeable. We knew that at no very distant date the war
would be upon us; but momentarily it was remote
and we were enjoying ourselves. In the time when
it was possible to get away from the station for a
couple of days, most of us motored up to Invermark
where Lord Dalhousie had kindly turned over his
shooting lodge to us. Here in the deep stillness of
the mountains it was possible to relax, and the war, if
it penetrated at all, was wafted up as the breath of the
vulgarity of another world. We shot grouse and
fished on the loch, and on one occasion after an
arduous day's stalking I shot a stag; but I am no
sportsman and the dying look in the beast's eyes
resolved me to confine my killing to Germans.

I was therefore relieved and grateful when Stapme
and Bubble let me in on their preciously guarded
secret. We three flew together and therefore had the
same time off. Stapme and Bubble would both come
up to Invermark, but neither of them shot. How they
employed their few hours of freedom will, I think,
come as a surprise to a number of people, for they
must have seemed from the outside as typical a pair

of easy-going pilots as one could expect to meet any-where. Stapme with his talk of beer, blokes, and carburettors, and Bubble with his absorption in things mechanical, might have been expected to spend their leaves, respectively, in a too fast car with a too loud blonde, and in getting together with the chaps in the local pub. In point of fact they played hide-and-seek with children.

Tarfside was a tiny hamlet a few miles down the road from Invermark, and to it this summer had come a dozen or so Scots children, evacuated from the more vulnerable towns in the district. They went to school at Brechin, a few miles from Montrose, but for the holidays they came to the mountains, under the care of Mrs. Davie, the admirable and unexacting mother of two of them. Their ages ranged from six to sixteen.

How Stapme and Bubble had first come upon them I never discovered, but from the moment that I saw those children I too was under their spell. That they really came from Brechin, that thin-blooded Wigan of the north, I was not prepared to admit ; kilted and tanned by the sun, they were so essentially *right* against that background of heather, burns, and pine. They were in no way precocious, but rather completely natural and unselfconscious. In the general confusion of introductions, one little fellow, the smallest, was left out. He approached me slowly with a grave face.

" I'm Rat Face," he said.

" How are you, Rat Face ? " I asked.

" Quite well, thank you. You can pick me up if you like."

I gave him a pick-a-back, and all day we played rounders, hide-and-seek, or picnicked, and as evening drew on we climbed up into the old hayloft and told stories, Stapme, Bubble, and I striving to outdo one another.

I lost my heart completely to Betty Davie, aged ten. She confided to me that I was her favourite, and I was ridiculously gratified. She was determined to be a school teacher, but with those eyes and the promise of those lips I did not doubt that her resolution would weaken.

It was with regret that we drove back to the aerodrome, and with a latent fear that we should not get back to Tarfside. We drove always straight to the Dispersal Point, each time expecting the greeting : " Tomorrow we move south." Out before the huts crouched our Spitfires, seemingly eager to be gone, the boldly painted names on their noses standing out in the gathering dusk. Nearly every plane was called by name, names as divergent as Boomerang, Valkyrie, and Angel Face. Mine I called Sredni Vashtar, after the immortal short story of Saki.

Sredni Vashtar was a ferret, worshipped and kept in the tool-shed by a little boy called Conradin : it finally made a meal of Conradin's most disagreeable

guardian, Mrs. De Ropp. Conradin in his worship
would chant this hymn :

Sredni Vashtar went forth,
His thoughts were red thoughts and his teeth were white,
His enemies called for peace, but he brought them death,
Sredni Vashtar the Beautiful.

I thought it appropriate.

The legend of the children at Tarfside soon spread
through the Squadron, and no three machines would
return from a practice flight without first sweeping in
tight formation low along the bed of the valley where
the children, grouped on a patch of grass by the road,
would wave and shout and dance in ecstasy.

Although our leaves did not coincide, I saw a fair
amount of Peter Pease but I found him exasperatingly
elusive. I had an urge to get behind that polite reserve,
and by drawing him into argument to discover how
his mind worked. The more reserved he was the
more sarcastically aggressive I became. It was to no
avail. I would throw him the ball and he would
quietly put it in his pocket. Whenever I thought I
had him cornered he would smilingly excuse himself
and retire to his rooms to write letters. What I did
not know, but might have guessed, was that he was
in love.

On occasion, however, we drove up to Aberdeen
to see Colin and had dinner together in the town.
Once Colin and I conspired to get him into some

dance hop. We both expressed an eagerness to go in, and rather than be awkward he agreed to go with us. The smell of humanity was oppressive, and we sat on the balcony watching the closely packed couples slowly circling the floor. A young woman, powerfully scented and with startlingly blond hair, was sitting next to me.

" You do look mournful," she said. " Come and have a dance."

I pointed apologetically to my foot and sighed :

" Twisted my ankle, I'm afraid, but my friend here is a good dancer."

I turned to Peter Pease and said, " I want you to meet Miss —— I'm sorry, I didn't get your name ? "

" McBride. Dolly, my friends call me."

" Miss McBride, Mr. Pease."

Peter got to his feet.

" I'm afraid I don't dance a tango very well, but I'd like to try."

They went off down the stairs, to appear a moment later on the floor. Colin and I craned our necks. Dolly was looking eagerly up at Peter and they were talking and laughing. At the end of the dance Peter led her from the floor, thanked her, and started back up the stairs.

" It's no good," said Colin mournfully. " I might have known : the laugh's on us."

I resented Peter's self-confidence, for while he was

shy, he was perfectly assured. I rather prided myself on my self-sufficiency, on my ability to be perfectly at ease with people of any standing or any age, but with Peter I felt, as it were, that at any moment he might discover me wearing a made-up tie. He would, of course, not be so tactless as to mention it, would in fact put himself out to be even more charming than before. But there it would be : no getting round it, the fellow knew. Well, damn it, why shouldn't I wear a made-up tie if I wanted to ?

I resented this assurance, basically because here was a man better orientated than I, and as the result of an upbringing and a system of education which I deeply distrusted and had in the past despised as being quite incapable of producing anything but, at the best, congenital idiots, and at the worst, fox-hunting bounders. For he was a product of the old-school-tie system in its most extreme form. He was more than comfortably off; his father owned property which in due course, as the eldest son, he would inherit ; he had been brought up in the orthodox Tory tradition and in the belief that this was as it should be.

I often attacked him and accused him of living in an ivory tower, but he refused to be drawn ; indeed there was little reason why he should be, for it was only too obvious that he was liked and respected by everyone in the Squadron. It was in fact almost impossible to draw him into an argument on any subject, though I tried everything, from apparently harmless conversation to attempts to make him lose his temper.

I wanted particularly to make him talk about the war, and in this I was determined to succeed. I knew that I need not expect any glib arguments. He was religious, and, I felt pretty certain, would not attempt to put forward any but the orthodox Christian views. Yet I wanted to hear his arguments from his own lips. I had an idea that the issue for him was an apprehension of something related to faith and not to any intellectual concept.

My chance came when we were sent down from Montrose to Edinburgh by train to fly up a couple of new Spitfires. We had the compartment to ourselves. I didn't temporize but asked him straight out his reasons for fighting the war. He gave me that slow smile of his.

"Well, Richard," he said, "you've got me at last, haven't you?"

He sat back in his corner and thought for a moment. Words didn't come easily to him, and I am bound to confess that in reconstructing his argument I do a certain violence to his expression. He was not as fluent as I shall make him. But what follows is at any rate the substance of his position.

"I don't know if I can answer you to your satisfaction," he said, "but I'll try. I would say that I was fighting the war to rid the world of fear — of the fear of fear is perhaps what I mean. If the Germans win this war, nobody except little Hitlers will dare do anything. England will be run as if it were a concentration camp, or at best a factory. All courage will die out of the world — the courage to love, to create, to take risks, whether physical or intellectual or moral. Men will hesitate to carry out the promptings of the heart or the brain because, having acted, they will live in fear that their action may be discovered and themselves cruelly punished. Thus all love, all spontaneity, will die out of the world. Emotion will have atrophied. Thought will have petrified. The oxygen breathed by the soul, so to speak, will vanish, and mankind will wither. Does that satisfy you ? "

" It's a good speech," I said, " but it's all big words. It's all negative. Isn't there something positive you want ? "

Peter flushed slightly. He who was the last person to clothe his feelings in big words had done so out of regard for me ; and I had reproached him. But he was persistent. What he had started he would finish.

" Something positive I want ? But of course. Only, saying what it is means big words again, confound you, Richard ! What I want is to see a better world come out of this war."

" What do you mean by *better* ? " I challenged him. " Christian, I suppose."

" Now who is using the big words ? " he wanted

to know. "You've used the biggest word of all. Yes,
Christian, of course. Nothing else. It isn't only that
I am a Christian by faith. It's that I don't know any
other way of life worth fighting for. Christianity
means to me, on the social plane, freedom, man's
humanity to man. Everything else I see as man's
inhumanity to man. I believe that we should all make
our contribution, even though it's a mere drop in the
ocean, to the betterment of humanity. I know that,
put into words, it sounds sentimental, and of course
you don't agree. I can see that."

I nodded. "You're quite right," I said. "I don't.
I think that your Christianity clouds the issue, makes
it harder to see what we're talking about. As I see it
there are three possible philosophies. First, there is
hedonism, living purely for pleasure. The rich, by
and large, did nothing but that here in England until
practically the other day — that is, the non-industrial
rich. And that life is over. Only the rich could live
that way, and now the poor aren't going to allow it any
longer. Secondly, one can live for the good of the community—or for the betterment of mankind, as you
would put it. Though how one is to be certain that
one's contribution *is* bettering humanity, God only
knows."

"Yes," Peter said, "He unquestionably does."

I threw up my hands. "There you go," I said.
"All you religious people are alike. In the end you

always fall back upon infallible faith. 'I feel it here,' you say, with a hand on your stomachs. Well, I may feel just the same thing ; but with me it's indigestion, or the exaltation I get from an hour of great music, or from Lear and Cordelia."

Peter stared out of the window. I was a little ashamed of that crack about the hand on the stomach. It smelled of Hyde Park oratory. And I could have gone on more easily if I felt that I had hurt him, or angered him. I knew that what was disturbing him was simply the distance between us, the gulf.

"Look at your missionary," I went on. "He goes off to Bunga Bunga land to convert the blacks to bowler hats and spats. He's quite certain that he has the call to dedicate himself to humanity. In point of fact he's probably putting into practice the third philosophy, the only one in which I can believe. That is, to live for the realization of one's self. Some do it by preaching, some by making love, others by building locomotives or smashing stock markets."

"If I gather what you mean," Peter said, "you mean something I should call rather base. In fact, I couldn't imagine a lower form of life. Can you be more explicit ?"

"Well," I said, "to be perfectly brutal about it — though actually it isn't in the least a brutal thing — I mean using the world as opposed to being used by the world. Every single artist who ever lived, every great scientist, did exactly that. You couldn't find a better example than Goethe, for instance, or Newton, or Leonardo. Would the world be poorer or richer if Goethe had been killed fighting for his native Frankfurt, or Leonardo had been stuck in the ribs by some petty Italian tyrant's lance ? Or if Einstein had been beaten to death by the Gestapo because his ' soul ' commanded that he fight for the Jewish peoples ? "

Peter, who was not ordinarily witty or mischievous, smiled almost maliciously.

" And is our Richard planning to be a Goethe or a Newton ? " he asked. Before I could break in he had gone on : " There was Joan of Arc, you know."

" You couldn't cite a better instance of what I mean," I said quickly. " Obsessed with self-realization, she was. The Voices were *her* voices, the king of France was *her* king, the French were *her* people. God ! What an egomaniac !

" But let me go on. You don't have to be a Goethe. I'm not concerned with genius. I'm concerned with my own potentialities. I say that I am fighting this war because I believe that, in war, one can swiftly develop all one's faculties to a degree it would normally take half a lifetime to achieve. And to do this, you must be as free from outside interference as possible. That's why I'm in the Air Force. For in a Spitfire we're back to war as it ought to be — if you can talk about war as it ought to be. Back to individual combat, to self-reliance, total responsibility for one's own fate. One either kills or is killed; and it's damned exciting. And after the war, when I shall be writing, I'll again be developing faster than the rest of you. Because a writer is constantly digging into himself, penetrating the life and nature of man, and thus realizing himself."

"Richard, I don't understand you," Peter said. "All your talk is hard-boiled; you as much as proclaim yourself a realist. And yet you are so fuzzy-minded as to assume that you'll be allowed to dig into yourself and the rest in a German-dominated world. You're not a medieval mystic, you know. You'll be able to think, perhaps, in a concentration camp, but not to write and impart what you think."

"Of course I won't. Don't take me for a bloody fool. Besides, we're agreed about the necessity for smashing the Germans. It's the purpose that we're arguing about. I want to smash them in order to be free to grow; you in order to be free to worship your God and lead your villagers in prayer."

"Suppose we go in to lunch," said Peter. "I could do with something to eat."

We made our way along to the dining-car, clambering over feet, kit-bags, and suitcases, tossed from compartment door to window and back again by the motion of the train. We were passing through rough river-scored mountains, deceptively clothed with a soft brown moss. "No place for a forced landing," I thought automatically.

The dining-car was full, one or two business men but mostly uniforms. We managed to get ourselves a couple of seats and I took a look at them. I wondered if these people asked themselves such questions as I was asking Peter — probably not, if what foreigners say about the English is true, that we hate thinking, analysis. Peter certainly did, and I left him alone through lunch.

When we had got back to our compartment Peter gave a sigh of content and settled back in the corner, happy in the belief that his ordeal was over. But I hadn't said the half of what was on my mind. I knew that I should surely never get such a chance at him again. So I started.

"Look here, Peter," I said. " Let's begin by agreeing that I am a selfish swine and am in the war only to get what I can out of it. But what about you? You're a landowner — a sort of dodo, a species nearly extinct. . . . No, don't stop me ! Even though you may not own half England, you're representative of the type. I'm quite ready to agree that you're not fighting to maintain the present system of land tenure. You're fighting for all the ideals you mentioned earlier. I know that. Do you expect to make the world a better place for your dependants to live in, solely through Christianity ; and if so, how ? "

Peter rather pointedly opened a window and stood staring out at the passing countryside. He was struggling to arrange his thoughts, to find words; and what he said came out so slowly, in such fragments of discourse, that I shall not attempt to give it shape. It was nothing new, and it came to this. He would be as decent to those in a less fortunate position as he possibly could, more especially to those dependent on him. He hoped that his rôle would consist in helping them, protecting them, keeping alive that ancient sturdy self-reliance of the true-born Englishman that had made England what she was.

About this I must say one thing. While Peter's words were all clichés on the surface, all copybook talk, underneath they were terrific. He was saying what was to him almost the most important thing he could say, something as intense as a prayer to his God. What he said was, if you like, stupidly English. But what he would *do*, the lengths to which he would go, the probity and charity with which he would live that extinct form of existence, would also be English; and magnificently English. Extinct is the word: Peter was the very parfit knyght.

I realized all this as he spoke, but I had no intention of pulling my punches because of it. " Well," said I, " if I had your altruism I'd try economics and not religion as my nostrum. I'd say to myself, we must do away with this unemployment, muck, undernourishment, and the rest of the horror that is the chief characteristic of every Christian State since Constantine became a Christian. And it differs from the non-Christian State only in that the others haven't been such raging persecutors of men of other faiths. Of course, there will still be what you'd call original sin. You still won't be able to prevent one man wanting to pop into bed with another man's wife. But on balance I should say you would be getting nearer to saving the world by economics than by religion, the greatest instrument of persecution ever devised."

"Oh, now wait a minute!" Peter protested. "I don't know much about either religion or economics, but I know this. Religious persecution has been periodic, but economic persecution has been constant, uninterrupted, never-ending. There's no evidence in history of men being better disposed towards one another because of economics, but there is some evidence of their being so through religion." Now he was on a subject he could warm to. Where he got his fresh eloquence from I don't know; but he went on more or less in this vein: "We're talking about two different things, you and I. You are talking about material misery and crime, and so on; whereas I am talking about something you're not interested in — sin, and the harm man does to himself. What I'm trying to say is this, that men who possess the religious sense know that you can't injure others without doing harm to yourself. You agree that there has always been economic misery. You're almost ready to admit it can't be altogether done away with. Well, make men Christians, I say, and they won't hurt others because they won't want to hurt themselves, their immortal souls."

It was queer how I, who had taken the offensive from the beginning, was now being put on the defensive by the conviction behind Peter's words. I was convinced, too; but I was not half as collected in that compartment as I am now, writing the debate out from memory. I recall that we rambled round the subject a good deal, and that Peter admitted he'd perhaps try to stand for Parliament. I pointed out to him that he would have either to vote with his Party on every issue — if there still was a dear old-fashioned Parliament — or retire a disappointed reformer. Suppose, I said, he turned out like Neville Chamberlain, acted as his conscience prompted and then found out he'd been a — well, never mind the epithet. I told him that as a writer I should be content to go my own way and be governed by any set of politicians he or his political enemies could dish up for the misguidance of the perhaps excessively patient British people.

But Peter had an answer to this. "Do you realize," he asked, "that your lofty political irresponsibilities are exactly what the Nazis are drilling into the German people ? You reject their system because you're an individualist and don't like taking orders. But if you are politically irresponsible, you have to take orders. I reject Nazism not only because I have a sense of history, but also because, unlike you, I believe its purpose is to stamp out the divine spark in Man."

We should be pulling into Edinburgh soon. I wasn't satisfied. Politics was an easier subject than the immortal soul, and I went back at him on that tack.

" How," I asked, " are you going to reconcile your moral and religious convictions with being a loyal Party member ? Especially if you were successful, and were taken into the Cabinet, some of the acts you committed in the name of the State would get you put away for life if you committed them as an individual."

" Now, Richard," Peter started to protest ; but I stopped him.

" No, no. Let me go on. In time of need — and politics are continuously in times of need — the rulers, the ruling classes, are always able to evoke exceptional circumstances and glibly plead the need of exceptional measures. They are for ever in a state of self-defence. You may define reform by saying that it indicates a weak state of ruling-class defence. Revolution you may define by saying that it represents the breakdown of ruling-class defence. You, as a Cabinet member, would spend your life defending a class interest — by a concession to the common people when the defences were weak, by a disguised persecution when your defences were strong. Yes, you would ! You wouldn't be able to help yourself. You'd be a cog in the Party machine — or, as I've hinted before, a mere overseer of your baronial acres who hadn't been able to stand the gaff in Whitehall."

My tirade had freshened me. I was feeling " fine," as Hemingway would say ; as fine as one of his heroes when a well-born girl offers him a bottle of precious brandy if only he will go to bed with her. Peter stared at me with a glint of curiosity in his eye. The day was darkening, and in the half-light his bony face had taken on a decidedly ascetic look, so that I felt more than ever in contact with an alien spiritual world.

" You're not a communist, Richard," he said —

" God knows I'm not ! "

" — but you are an anarchist."

" Nonsense ! " said I. " It's simpler than that. You are going to concern yourself with politics and mankind when the war is over : I am going to concern myself with the individual and Richard Hillary. I may or may not be exactly a man of my time : I don't know. But I know that you are an anachronism. In an age when to love one's country is vulgar, to love God archaic, and to love mankind sentimental, you do all three. If you can work out a harmonious synthesis, I'll take my hat off to you. The really funny thing is that I, as an individual, shall certainly do less harm to the world writing than you as a Party member, a governor of the nation, are bound to do in office."

"That," said Peter, "is most certainly not true. I don't read much myself; but lots of people round me do. And the harm done them by their reading these past few years has been absolutely appalling. It is taking this war to correct the flubdub of the 1920s' pacifism. All due to writers! Was there a single poet in Oxford who didn't write surrealist economics, who didn't proclaim that he refused to fight for king and country, instead of sticking to his cuckoos and bluebells? Not one! Besides, wasn't it your friend Goethe who said that while an artist never writes with a moral end in view, the effect of a work of art is always moral?"

"Yes, my good Peter," I said. "But that's where I have you, because I don't care. The mass of mankind leaves me cold. My only concern outside myself is my immediate circle of friends, to whom I behave well, basically, I suppose, because I hope they'll behave well towards me. That's merely oiling the wheels of an agreeable existence. Thus if I were asked to contribute to a friend of mine about to go down from Oxford through lack of money I would do so willingly, but if I were asked to subscribe to some African chief's wife because she was being beaten up by her husband I should refuse as I wouldn't know the good lady. But that in effect is what you're asking us all to do."

" Oh, but you're such a fraud, Richard," he said cheerfully. " What about those children at Tarf-side ? "

" For God's sake," I said, " they gave me more pleasure than I gave them. I was taking, not giving."

Peter groaned.

" I know, I know," I said. " You are about to tell me that in time, looking at the world and its featherless bipeds, studying the machinery that ani-mates them, and describing it, I shall grow very fond of them. I shall end up with whiskers and a rage for primitive Christianity, like Tolstoi ; or bald and sitting in homespuns among my worshippers, like Gandhi. But I shan't, and if you live long enough I'll prove it to you."

Peter said : " I can see that neither of us is going to convince the other. And I don't mind at all admitting that I am sure you will change your tune. It won't be long either. Something bigger than you and me is coming out of this, and as it grows you'll grow with it. Your preconceived notions won't last long. You are not entirely unfeeling, Richard. I'm sure it needs only some psychological shock, some affront to your sensibility, to arouse your pity or your anger sufficiently to make you forget yourself."

"I doubt it," I said ; and at that we left it.

We spent the night at Turnhouse, collected the two Spitfires and flew back to Montrose. Before I had switched off, Bubble was climbing up on to the wing.

"Get your things packed and hand them over to Sergeant Ross. We're on our way. You'd left before we could stop you."

It had come at last. The whole Squadron was moving down to Turnhouse. That was only Edinburgh, but with the German offensive in full swing in the south, it could mean only one thing. In a very few days we should be further south and in it. Broody Benson was hopping up and down like a madman.

"Now we'll show the bastards ! Jesus, will we show 'em !"

Stapme was capering about shaking everyone by the hand, and Raspberry's moustache looked as though it would fall off with excitement. "Eh, now they'll cop it and no mistake," he chortled. "I've had just about enough of bulling about up here !" Even Boulter was out of bed, his ears twitching uncontrollably. Our relief Squadron was already coming in, plane after plane engining down over the boundary. Rusty quickly allocated us to sections and "B" Flight roared twelve strong across the aerodrome, dipped once over the Mess, and headed south.

For a moment I thought Rusty had forgotten, but
then I heard his voice down the R.T., " Once more,
boys," and in four sections of three we were banking
to starboard and headed for the mountains.

They had heard the news, and as we went into
line astern and dived one by one in salute over the
valley, none of the children moved or shouted. With
white boulders they had spelt out on the road the two
words : " Good Luck."

We rejoined formation and once again headed
south. I looked back. The children stood close
together on the grass, their hands raised in silent
farewell.

# 5

# *The Invaders*

AFTER kicking our heels for two days at Turnhouse, a reaction set in. We were like children with the promise of a trip to the seaside, broken because of rain. On the third day I allowed myself to be persuaded against my better judgment to take up a gun again.

The Duke of Hamilton, the Station C.O., had offered the Squadron a couple of days grouse-shooting on his estate. Colin, of course, was eager to go as were two other "A" Flight pilots, Sheep Gilroy and Black Morton. Sheep was a Scotsman and a farmer, with a port-wine complexion and features which gave rise to his name. I finally agreed to go in place of Peter Pease, who was on duty, and the four of us set off. It was pouring with rain when we arrived, to be greeted by the usual intimidating band of beaters, loaders, gillies, and what-not. We set off at once for the butts, an uphill climb across the moors of a mere couple of miles, the others apparently in no way put out by the weather. We climbed in single file, I bringing up the protesting rear, miserable, wet, and muddy from repeated falls into the heather. After about an hour we reached the top and disposed ourselves in four butts, while the beaters, loaders, gillies, and what-not squelched away into the mist. After the first half-hour, during which my hands turned blue and my feet lost all feeling, I sat down and resigned myself to the sensation of the wet earth steadily seeping through my breeches. From time to time I got up and looked over at the others, alert, guns gripped firmly, staring eagerly into the mist, and I was ashamed of my craven spirit : I chid myself. Were there not gentlemen — and the right type of gentlemen too — who paid £30 a day for the privilege of just such suffering ? My musings were interrupted by a series of animal cries, and from out of the mist emerged the beaters, beating. As a result of this lengthy coordination of effort one hare and two rather tired-looking birds put in an apologetic short-lived appearance, to be summarily dispatched by our withering fire. The prospect of lunch cheered me, and my hunger was such that I was undismayed at the thought of the long walk back, but my illusions were rudely shattered when we set off purposefully for a second lot of butts where a larger flock, flight, covey, or what-have-you was expected. Once again the beaters vanished into the mist, once again we were left damply to our meditations, and once again a discreet flutter of wings rewarded our vigil. This time my cries of hunger were accorded a grudging attention and we set off for the brake, parked some miles away and containing whisky and sandwiches. Sheep and Black Morton had to return to Turnhouse that evening for duty, but Colin and I were to stay overnight and shoot again in the morning (on condition it wasn't raining). Back at the Lodge I got out of my wet clothes and sank gratefully into a hot bath, allowing the steam to waft away the more acute memories of the day's discomforts. Colin at dinner stretched out his legs contentedly, and his face wore the rapt expression of the madman who, when asked why he banged his head against the wall, replied that it was such fun when he stopped.

We retired early to bed and slept until, at two o'clock in the morning, a gillie banged on the door. Colin got up, took from the gillie's hand a telegram, opened it, and read it aloud. It said: " SQUADRON MOVING SOUTH STOP CAR WILL FETCH YOU AT EIGHT OCLOCK DENHOLM." For us, the war began that night.

At ten o'clock we were back at Turnhouse. The rest of the Squadron were all set to leave ; we were to move down to Hornchurch, an aerodrome twelve miles east of London on the Thames Estuary. Four machines would not be serviceable until the evening, and Broody Benson, Pip Cardell, Colin, and I were to fly them down. We took off at four o'clock, some

five hours after the others, Broody leading, Pip and
I to each side, and Colin in the box, map-reading.
Twenty-four of us flew south that tenth day of
August 1940 : of those twenty-four eight were to
fly back.

We landed at Hornchurch at about seven o'clock
to receive our first shock. Instead of one section
there were four Squadrons at readiness ; 603 Squadron were already in action. They started coming in
about half an hour after we landed, smoke stains along
the leading edges of the wings showing that all the
guns had been fired. They had acquitted themselves
well although caught at a disadvantage of height.

"You don't have to look for them," said Brian.
"You have to look for a way out."

From this flight Don MacDonald did not return.

At this time the Germans were sending over comparatively few bombers. They were making a
determined attempt to wipe out our entire Fighter
Force, and from dawn till dusk the sky was filled with
Messerschmitt 109's and 110's.

Half a dozen of us always slept over at the Dispersal Hut to be ready for a surprise enemy attack at
dawn. This entailed being up by four-thirty and by
five o'clock having our machines warmed up and the
oxygen, sights, and ammunition tested. The first
Hun attack usually came over about breakfast-time
and from then until eight o'clock at night we were

almost continuously in the air. We ate when we could, baked beans and bacon and eggs being sent over from the Mess.

On the morning after our arrival I walked over with Peter Howes and Broody. Howes was at Hornchurch with another Squadron and worried because he had as yet shot nothing down. Every evening when we came into the Mess he would ask us how many we had got and then go over miserably to his room. His Squadron had had a number of losses and was due for relief. If ever a man needed it, it was Howes. Broody, on the other hand, was in a high state of excitement, his sharp eager face grinning from ear to ear. We left Howes at his Dispersal Hut and walked over to where our machines were being warmed up. The voice of the controller came unhurried over the loud-speaker, telling us to take off, and in a few seconds we were running for our machines. I climbed into the cockpit of my plane and felt an empty sensation of suspense in the pit of my stomach. For one second time seemed to stand still and I stared blankly in front of me. I knew that that morning I was to kill for the first time. That I might be killed or in any way injured did not occur to me. Later, when we were losing pilots regularly, I did consider it in an abstract way when on the ground; but once in the air, never. I knew it could not happen to me. I suppose every pilot knows that, knows it cannot happen to him ; even when he is taking off for the last time, when he will not return, he knows that he cannot be killed. I wondered idly what he was like, this man I would kill. Was he young, was he fat, would he die with the Fuehrer's name on his lips, or would he die alone, in that last moment conscious of himself as a man ? I would never know. Then I was being strapped in, my mind automatically checking the controls, and we were off.

We ran into them at 18,000 feet, twenty yellow-nosed Messerschmitt 109's, about 500 feet above us. Our Squadron strength was eight, and as they came down on us we went into line astern and turned head on to them. Brian Carbury, who was leading the Section, dropped the nose of his machine, and I could almost feel the leading Nazi pilot push forward on his stick to bring his guns to bear. At the same moment Brian hauled hard back on his own control stick and led us over them in a steep climbing turn to the left. In two vital seconds they lost their advantage. I saw Brian let go a burst of fire at the leading plane, saw the pilot put his machine into a half roll, and knew that he was mine. Automatically, I kicked the rudder to the left to get him at right angles, turned the gun-button to " Fire," and let go in a four-second burst with full deflection. He came right through my sights and I saw the tracer from all eight guns thud home. For a second he seemed to hang motionless ; then a jet of red flame shot upwards and he spun out of sight.

For the next few minutes I was too busy looking after myself to think of anything, but when, after a short while, they turned and made off over the Channel, and we were ordered to our base, my mind began to work again.

It had happened.

My first emotion was one of satisfaction, satisfaction at a job adequately done, at the final logical conclusion of months of specialized training. And then I had a feeling of the essential rightness of it all. He was dead and I was alive ; it could so easily have been the other way round ; and that would somehow have been right too. I realized in that moment just how lucky a fighter pilot is. He has none of the personalized emotions of the soldier, handed a rifle and bayonet and told to charge. He does not even have to share the dangerous emotions of the bomber pilot who night after night must experience that childhood longing for smashing things. The fighter pilot's emotions are those of the duellist — cool, precise, impersonal. He is privileged to kill well. For if one must either kill or be killed, as now one must, it should, I feel, be done with dignity. Death should be given the setting it deserves ; it should never be a pettiness ; and for the fighter pilot it never can be.

From this flight Broody Benson did not return.

During that August-September period we were always so outnumbered that it was practically impossible, unless we were lucky enough to have the advantage of height, to deliver more than one Squadron attack. After a few seconds we always broke up, and the sky was a smoke trail of individual dog-fights. The result was that the Squadron would come home individually, machines landing one after the other at intervals of about two minutes. After an hour, Uncle George would make a check-up on who was missing. Often there would be a telephone-call from some pilot to say that he had made a forced landing at some other aerodrome, or in a field. But the telephone wasn't always so welcome. It would be a rescue squad announcing the number of a crashed machine ; then Uncle George would check it, and cross another name off the list. At that time, the losing of pilots was somehow extremely impersonal ; nobody, I think, felt any great emotion — there simply wasn't time for it.

After the hard lesson of the first two days, we became more canny and determined not to let ourselves be caught from above. We would fly on the reciprocal of the course given us by the controller until we got to 15,000 feet, and then fly back again, climbing all the time. By this means we usually saw the Huns coming in below us, and were in a perfect position to deliver a Squadron attack. If caught at a disadvantage, they would never stay to fight, but always turned straight back for the Channel. We arranged a system whereby two pilots always flew together — thus if one should follow a plane down the other stayed 500 feet or so above, to protect him from attack in the rear.

Often machines would come back to their base just long enough for the ground staff, who worked with beautiful speed, to refuel them and put in a new oxygen bottle and more ammunition before taking off again. Uncle George was shot down several times but always turned up unhurt ; once we thought Rusty was gone for good, but he was back leading his flight the next day ; one sergeant pilot in " A " Flight was shot down four times, but he seemed to bear a charmed life.

The sun and the great height at which we flew often made it extremely difficult to pick out the enemy machines, but it was here that Sheep's experience on the moors of Scotland proved invaluable. He always led the guard section and always saw the Huns long before anyone else. For me the sun presented a major problem. We had dark lenses on our glasses, but I, as I have mentioned before, never wore mine. They gave me a feeling of claustrophobia. With spots on the wind-screen, spots before the eyes, and a couple of spots which might be Messerschmitts, blind spots on my goggles seemed too much of a good thing ; I always slipped them up on to my forehead before going into action. For this and for not wearing gloves I paid a stiff price.

I remember once going practically to France before shooting down a 109. There were two of them, flying at sea-level and headed for the French coast. Raspberry was flying beside me and caught one half-way across. I got right up close behind the second one and gave it a series of short bursts. It darted about in front, like a startled rabbit, and finally plunged into the sea about three miles off the French coast.

On another occasion I was stupid enough actually to fly over France : the sky appeared to be perfectly clear but for one returning Messerschmitt, flying very high. I had been trying to catch him for about ten minutes and was determined that he should not get away. Eventually I caught him inland from Calais and was just about to open fire when I saw a squadron of twelve Messerschmitts coming in on my right. I was extremely frightened, but turned in towards them and opened fire at the leader. I could see his tracer going past underneath me, and then I saw his hood fly off, and the next moment they were past. I didn't wait to see any more, but made off for home, pursued for half the distance by eleven very determined Germans. I landed a good hour after everyone else to find Uncle George just finishing his check-up.

From this flight Larry Cunningham did not return. After about a week of Hornchurch, I woke late one morning to the noise of machines running up on the aerodrome. It irritated me : I had a headache.

Having been on every flight the previous day, the morning was mine to do with as I pleased. I got up slowly, gazed dispassionately at my tongue in the mirror, and wandered over to the Mess for breakfast. It must have been getting on for twelve o'clock when I came out on to the aerodrome to find the usual August heat haze forming a dull pall over everything. I started to walk across the aerodrome to the Dispersal Point on the far side. There were only two machines on the ground so I concluded that the Squadron was already up. Then I heard a shout, and our ground crew drew up in a lorry beside me. Sergeant Ross leaned out :

" Want a lift, sir ? We're going round."

" No, thanks, Sergeant. I'm going to cut across."

This was forbidden for obvious reasons, but I felt like that.

" O.K., sir. See you round there."

The lorry trundled off down the road in a cloud of dust. I walked on across the landing ground. At that moment I heard the emotionless voice of the controller.

" Large enemy bombing formation approaching Hornchurch. All personnel not engaged in active duty take cover immediately."

I looked up. They were still not visible. At the
Dispersal Point I saw Bubble and Pip Cardell make
a dash for the shelter. Three Spitfires just landed,
turned about and came past me with a roar to take
off down-wind. Our lorry was still trundling along
the road, maybe half-way round, and seemed suddenly an awfully long way from the Dispersal Point.

I looked up again, and this time I saw them —
about a dozen slugs, shining in the bright sun and
coming straight on. At the rising scream of the first
bomb I instinctively shrugged up my shoulders and
ducked my head. Out of the corner of my eye I saw
the three Spitfires. One moment they were about
twenty feet up in close formation ; the next cata-
pulted apart as though on elastic. The leader went
over on his back and ploughed along the runway with
a rending crash of tearing fabric ; No. 2 put a wing
in and spun round on his airscrew, while the plane
on the left was blasted wingless into the next field.
I remember thinking stupidly, " That's the shortest
flight he's ever taken," and then my feet were nearly
knocked from under me, my mouth was full of dirt,
and Bubble, gesticulating like a madman from the
shelter entrance, was yelling, " Run, you bloody fool,
run ! " I ran. Suddenly awakened to the lunacy of
my behaviour, I covered the distance to that shelter
as if impelled by a rocket and shot through the entrance while once again the ground rose up and hit

me, and my head smashed hard against one of the pillars. I subsided on a heap of rubble and massaged it.

"Who's here?" I asked, peering through the gloom.

"Cardell and I and three of our ground crew," said Bubble, "and, by the Grace of God, you!"

I could see by his mouth that he was still talking, but a sudden concentration of the scream and crump of falling bombs made it impossible to hear him.

The air was thick with dust and the shelter shook and heaved at each explosion, yet somehow held firm. For about three minutes the bedlam continued, and then suddenly ceased. In the utter silence which followed nobody moved. None of us wished to be the first to look on the devastation which we felt must be outside. Then Bubble spoke. "Praise God!" he said, "I'm not a civilian. Of all the bloody frightening things I've ever done, sitting in that shelter was the worst. Me for the air from now on!"

It broke the tension and we scrambled out of the entrance. The runways were certainly in something of a mess. Gaping holes and great gobbets of earth were everywhere. Right in front of us a bomb had landed by my Spitfire, covering it with a shower of grit and rubble.

I turned to the aircraftsman standing beside me. "Will you get hold of Sergeant Ross and tell him to have a crew give her an inspection."

He jerked his head towards one corner of the aerodrome: "I think I'd better collect the crew myself, sir. Sergeant Ross won't be doing any more inspections."

I followed his glance and saw the lorry, the roof about twenty yards away, lying grotesquely on its side. I climbed into the cockpit, and, feeling faintly sick, tested out the switches. Bubble poked his head over the side.

"Let's go over to the Mess and see what's up: all our machines will be landing down at the reserve landing field, anyway."

I climbed out and walked over to find that the three Spitfire pilots were quite unharmed but for a few superficial scratches, in spite of being machine-gunned by the bombers. "Operations" was undamaged: no hangar had been touched and the Officers' Mess had two windows broken.

The Station Commander ordered every available man and woman on to the job of repairing the aerodrome surface and by four o'clock there was not a hole to be seen. Several unexploded bombs were marked off, and two lines of yellow flags were laid down to mark the runways. At five o'clock our Squadron, taking off for a "flap" from the reserve field, landed without incident on its home base. Thus, apart from four men killed in the lorry and a network of holes on the landing surface, there was nothing to show for ten minutes' really accurate bombing from 12,000 feet, in which several dozen sticks of bombs had been dropped. It was a striking proof of the inefficacy of their attempts to wipe out our advance fighter aerodromes.

Brian had a bullet through his foot, and as my machine was still out of commission, I took his place in readiness for the next show. I had had enough of the ground for one day.

Six o'clock came and went, and no call. We started to play poker and I was winning. It was agreed that we should stop at seven : should there be a " flap " before then, the game was off. I gazed anxiously at the clock. I am always unlucky at cards, but when the hands pointed to 6.55 I really began to feel my luck was on the change. But sure enough at that moment came the voice of the controller : " 603 Squadron take off and patrol base : further instructions in the air."

We made a dash for our machines and within two minutes were off the ground. Twice we circled the aerodrome to allow all twelve planes to get in formation. We were flying in four sections of three : Red Section leading, Blue and Green to right and left, and the three remaining planes forming a guard section above and behind us.

I was flying No. 2 in the Blue Section.

Over the radio came the voice of the controller :

" Hullo, Red Leader," followed by instructions on course and height.

As always, for the first few minutes we flew on the reciprocal of the course given until we reached 15,000 feet. We then turned about and flew on 110° in an all-out climb, thus coming out of the sun and gaining height all the way.

During the climb Uncle George was in constant touch with the ground. We were to intercept about twenty enemy fighters at 25,000 feet. I glanced across at Stapme and saw his mouth moving. That meant he was singing again. He would sometimes do this with his radio set on " send," with the result that, mingled with our instructions from the ground, we would hear a raucous rendering of " Night and Day." And then quite clearly over the radio I heard the Germans excitedly calling to each other. This was a not infrequent occurrence and it made one feel that they were right behind, although often they were some distance away. I switched my set to " send " and called out " *Halt's Maul !* " and as many other choice pieces of German invective as I could remember. To my delight I heard one of them answer : " You feelthy Englishmen, we will teach you how to speak to a German." I am aware that this sounds a tall story, but several others in the Squadron were listening out and heard the whole thing.

I looked down. It was a completely cloudless sky

and way below lay the English countryside, stretching lazily into the distance, a quite extraordinary picture of green and purple in the setting sun.

I took a glance at my altimeter. We were at 28,000 feet. At that moment Sheep yelled " Tallyho " and dropped down in front of Uncle George in a slow dive in the direction of the approaching planes. Uncle George saw them at once.

" O.K.   Line astern."

I drew in behind Stapme and took a look at them. They were about 2000 feet below us, which was a pleasant change, but they must have spotted us at the same moment, for they were forming a protective circle, one behind the other, which is a defence formation hard to break.

" Echelon starboard " came Uncle George's voice.

We spread out fanwise to the right.

" Going down ! "

One after the other we peeled off in a power dive. I picked out one machine and switched my gun-button to " Fire." At 300 yards I had him in my sights. At 200 I opened up in a long four-second burst and saw the tracer going into his nose. Then I was pulling out, so hard that I could feel my eyes dropping through my neck. Coming round in a slow climbing turn, I saw that we had broken them up. The sky was now a mass of individual dog-fights. Several of them had already been knocked down. One I hoped was mine, but on pulling up I had not been able to see the result. To my left I saw Peter Pease make a head-on attack on a Messerschmitt. They were headed straight for each other and it looked as though the fire of both was striking home. Then at the last moment the Messerschmitt pulled up, taking Peter's fire full in the belly. It rolled on to its back, yellow flames pouring from the cockpit, and vanished.

The next few minutes were typical. First the sky a bedlam of machines ; then suddenly silence and not a plane to be seen. I noticed then that I was very tired and very hot. The sweat was running down my face in rivulets. But this was no time for vague reflections. Flying around the sky on one's own at that time was not a healthy course of action.

I still had some ammunition left. Having no desire to return to the aerodrome until it had all been used to some good purpose, I took a look around the sky for some friendly fighters. About a mile away over Dungeness I saw a formation of about forty Hurricanes on patrol at 20,000 feet. Feeling that there was safety in numbers, I set off in their direction. When about 200 yards from the rear machine, I looked down and saw 5000 feet below another formation of fifty machines flying in the same direction. Flying stepped up like this was an old trick of the Huns, and I was glad to see we were adopting the same tactics. But as though hit by a douche of cold water, I suddenly woke up. There were far more machines flying together than we could ever muster over one spot. I took another look at the rear machine in my formation, and sure enough, there was the Swastika on its tail. Yet they all seemed quite oblivious of my presence. I had the sun behind me and a glorious opportunity. Closing in to 150 yards I let go a three-second burst into the rear machine. It flicked on to its back and spun out of sight. Feeling like an irresponsible schoolboy who has perpetrated some crime which must inevitably be found out, I glanced round me. Still nobody seemed disturbed. I suppose I could have repeated the performance on the next machine, but I felt that it was inadvisable to tempt Providence too far. I did a quick half roll and made off home, where I found to my irritation that Raspberry, as usual, had three planes down to my one.

There was to be a concert on the Station that night, but as I had to be up at five the next morning for Dawn Readiness, I had a quick dinner and two beers, and went to bed, feeling not unsatisfied with the day.

Perhaps the most amusing though painful experience which I had was when I was shot down acting as Arse-end Charlie to a Squadron of Hurricanes. Arse-end Charlie is the man who weaves backwards and forwards above and behind the Squadron to protect them from attack from the rear. There had been the usual dog-fights over the South Coast, and the

Squadron had broken up. Having only fired one snap burst, I climbed up in search of friendly Spitfires, but found instead a Squadron of Hurricanes flying round the sky at 18,000 feet in sections of stepped-up threes, but with no rear-guard. So I joined on. I learned within a few seconds the truth of the old warning, " Beware of the Hun in the Sun." I was making pleasant little sweeps from side to side, and peering earnestly into my mirror when, from out of the sun and dead astern, bullets started appearing along my port wing. There is an appalling tendency to sit and watch this happen without taking any action, as though mesmerized by a snake ; but I managed to pull myself together and go into a spin, at the same time attempting to call up the Hurricanes and warn them, but I found that my radio had been shot away. At first there appeared to be little damage done and I started to climb up again, but black smoke began pouring out of the engine and there was an unpleasant smell of escaping glycol. I thought I had better get home while I could ; but as the wind-screen was soon covered with oil I realized that I couldn't make it and decided instead to put down at Lympne, where there was an aerodrome. Then I realized that I wasn't going to make Lympne either — I was going at full boost and only clocking 90 miles per hour, so I decided that I had better put down in the nearest field before I stalled and spun in. I chose a cornfield and put the machine down on its belly. Fortunately nothing caught fire, and I had just climbed out and switched off the petrol, when to my amazement I saw an ambulance coming through the gate. This I thought was real service, until the corporal and two orderlies who climbed out started cantering away in the opposite direction, their necks craned up to the heavens. I looked up and saw about 50 yards away a parachute, and suspended on the end, his legs dangling vaguely, Colin. He was a little burned about his face and hands but quite cheerful.

We were at once surrounded by a bevy of officers and discovered that we had landed practically in the back garden of a Brigade cocktail party. A salvage crew from Lympne took charge of my machine, a doctor took charge of Colin, and the rest took charge of me, handing me double whiskies for the nerves at a laudable rate. I was put up that night by the Brigadier, who thought I was suffering from a rather severe shock, largely because by dinner-time I was so pie-eyed that I didn't dare open my mouth but answered all his questions with a glassy stare. The next day I went up to London by train, a somewhat incongruous figure, carrying a helmet and parachute. The prospect of a long and tedious journey by tube to Hornchurch did not appeal to me, so I called up the Air Ministry and demanded a car and a W.A.A.F. I was put on to the good lady in charge of transport, a sergeant, who protested apologetically that she must have the authorization of a Wing Commander. I told her forcibly that at this moment I was considerably more important than any Wing Commander, painted a vivid picture of the complete disorganization of Fighter Command in the event of my not being back at Hornchurch within an hour, and clinched the argument by telling her that my parachute was a military secret which must on no account be seen in a train. By the afternoon I was flying again.

That evening there was a terrific attack on Hornchurch and, for the first time since coming south, I saw some bombers. There were twelve Dornier 215's flying in close formation at about 12,000 feet, and headed back for France. I was on my way back to the aerodrome when I first sighted them about 5000 feet below me. I dived straight down in a quarter head-on attack. It seemed quite impossible to miss, and I pressed the button. Nothing happened ; I had already fired all my ammunition. I could not turn back, so I put both my arms over my head and went straight through the formation, never thinking I'd get out of it unscratched. I landed on the aerodrome with the machine, quite serviceable, but a little draughty.

From this flight Bubble Waterston did not return.

And so August drew to a close with no slackening of pressure in the enemy offensive. Yet the Squadron showed no signs of strain, and I personally was content.

This was what I had waited for, waited for nearly a year, and I was not disappointed. If I felt anything, it was a sensation of relief. We had little time to think, and each day brought new action. No one thought of the future : sufficient unto the day was the emotion thereof. At night one switched off one's mind like an electric light.

It was one week after Bubble went that I crashed into the North Sea.

BOOK TWO

# 6

## Shall I Live for a Ghost?

I WAS falling. Falling slowly through a dark pit. I was dead. My body, headless, circled in front of me. I saw it with my mind, my mind that was the redness in front of the eye, the dull scream in the ear, the grinning of the mouth, the skin crawling on the skull. It was death and resurrection. Terror, moving with me, touched my cheek with hers and I felt the flesh wince. Faster, faster. . . . I was hot now, hot, again one with my body, on fire and screaming soundlessly. Dear God, no! No! Not that, not again. The sickly smell of death was in my nostrils and a confused roar of sound. Then all was quiet. I was back.

Someone was holding my arms.

"Quiet now. There's a good boy. You're going to be all right. You've been very ill and you mustn't talk."

I tried to reach up my hand but could not.

"Is that you, nurse? What have they done to me?"

"Well, they've put something on your face and

157

hands to stop them hurting and you won't be able to see for a little while. But you mustn't talk : you're not strong enough yet."

Gradually I realized what had happened. My face and hands had been scrubbed and then sprayed with tannic acid. The acid had formed into a hard black cement. My eyes alone had received different treatment : they were coated with a thick layer of gentian violet. My arms were propped up in front of me, the fingers extended like witches' claws, and my body was hung loosely on straps just clear of the bed.

I can recollect no moments of acute agony in the four days which I spent in that hospital ; only a great sea of pain in which I floated almost with comfort. Every three hours I was injected with morphia, so while imagining myself quite coherent, I was for the most part in a semi-stupor. The memory of it has remained a confused blur.

Two days without eating, and then periodic doses of liquid food taken through a tube. An appalling thirst, and hundreds of bottles of ginger beer. Being blind, and not really feeling strong enough to care. Imagining myself back in my plane, unable to get out, and waking to find myself shouting and bathed in sweat. My parents coming down to see me and their wonderful self-control.

They arrived in the late afternoon of my second

day in bed, having with admirable restraint done nothing the first day. On the morning of the crash my mother had been on her way to the Red Cross, when she felt a premonition that she must go home. She told the taxi-driver to turn about and arrived at the flat to hear the telephone ringing. It was our Squadron Adjutant, trying to reach my father. Embarrassed by finding himself talking to my mother, he started in on a glamorized history of my exploits in the air and was bewildered by my mother cutting him short to ask where I was. He managed somehow after about five minutes of incoherent stuttering to get over his news.

They arrived in the afternoon and were met by Matron. Outside my ward a twittery nurse explained that they must not expect to find me looking quite normal, and they were ushered in. The room was in darkness ; I just a dim shape in one corner. Then the blinds were shot up, all the lights switched on, and there I was. As my mother remarked later, the performance lacked only the rolling of drums and a spotlight. For the sake of decorum my face had been covered with white gauze, with a slit in the middle through which protruded my lips.

We spoke little, my only coherent remark being that I had no wish to go on living if I were to look like Alice. Alice was a large country girl who had once been our maid. As a child she had been burned and disfigured by a Primus stove. I was not aware that she had made any impression on me, but now I was unable to get her out of my mind. It was not so much her looks as her smell I had continually in my nostrils and which I couldn't dissociate from the disfigurement.

They sat quietly and listened to me rambling for an hour. Then it was time for my dressings and they took their leave.

The smell of ether. Matron once doing my dressing with three orderlies holding my arms; a nurse weeping quietly at the head of the bed, and no remembered sign of a doctor. A visit from the lifeboat crew that had picked me up, and a terrible longing to make sense when talking to them. Their inarticulate sympathy and assurance of quick recovery. Their discovery that an ancestor of mine had founded the lifeboats, and my pompous and unsolicited promise of a subscription. The expectation of an American ambulance to drive me up to the Masonic Hospital (for Margate was used only as a clearing station). Believing that I was already in it and on my way, and waking to the disappointment that I had not been moved. A dream that I was fighting to open my eyes and could not : waking in a sweat to realize it was a dream and then finding it to be true. A sensation of time slowing down, of words and actions, all in slow motion. Sweat, pain, smells, cheering messages from the Squadron, and an overriding apathy.

Finally I was moved. The ambulance appeared with a cargo of two somewhat nervous A.T.S. women who were to drive me to London, and, with my nurse in attendance, and wrapped in an old grandmother's shawl, I was carried aboard and we were off. For the first few miles I felt quite well, dictated letters to my nurse, drank bottle after bottle of ginger beer, and gossiped with the drivers. They described the country-side for me, told me they were new to the job, expressed satisfaction at having me for a consignment, asked me if I felt fine. Yes, I said, I felt fine; asked my nurse if the drivers were pretty, heard her answer yes, heard them simpering, and we were all very matey. But after about half an hour my arms began to throb from the rhythmical jolting of the road. I stopped dictating, drank no more ginger beer, and didn't care whether they were pretty or not. Then they lost their way. Wasn't it awful and shouldn't they stop and ask? No, they certainly shouldn't: they could call out the names of the streets and I would tell them where to go. By the time we arrived at Ravenscourt Park I was pretty much all-in. I was carried into the hospital and once again felt the warm September sun burning my face. I was put in a private ward and had the impression of a hundred excited ants buzzing around me. My nurse said good-bye and started to sob. For no earthly reason I found myself in tears. It had been a lousy hospital, I had never seen the nurse anyway, and I was now in very good hands; but I suppose I was in a fairly exhausted state. So there we all were, snivelling about the place and getting nowhere. Then the charge nurse came up and took my arm and asked me what my name was.

"Dick," I said.

"Ah," she said brightly. "We must call you Richard the Lion Heart."

I made an attempt at a polite laugh but all that came out was a dismal groan and I fainted away. The house surgeon took the opportunity to give me an anaesthetic and removed all the tannic acid from my left hand.

At this time tannic acid was the recognized treatment for burns. The theory was that in forming a hard cement it protected the skin from the air, and encouraged it to heal up underneath. As the tannic started to crack, it was to be chipped off gradually with a scalpel, but after a few months of experience, it was discovered that nearly all pilots with third-degree burns so treated developed secondary infection and septicaemia. This caused its use to be discontinued and gave us the dubious satisfaction of knowing that we were suffering in the cause of science. Both my hands were suppurating, and the fingers were already contracting under the tannic and curling down into the palms. The risk of shock was considered too great for them to do both hands. I must have been under the anaesthetic for about fifteen minutes and in that time I saw Peter Pease killed.

He was after another machine, a tall figure leaning slightly forward with a smile at the corner of his mouth. Suddenly from nowhere a Messerschmitt was on his tail about 150 yards away. For two seconds nothing happened. I had a terrible feeling of futility. Then at the top of my voice I shouted, " Peter, for God's sake look out behind ! "

I saw the Messerschmitt open up and a burst of fire hit Peter's machine. His expression did not change, and for a moment his machine hung motion-less. Then it turned slowly on its back and dived to the ground. I came-to, screaming his name, with two nurses and the doctor holding me down on the bed.

" All right now. Take it easy, you're not dead yet. That must have been a very bad dream."

I said nothing. There wasn't anything to say. Two days later I had a letter from Colin. My nurse read it to me. It was very short, hoping that I was getting better and telling me that Peter was dead.

Slowly I came back to life. My morphia injections were less frequent and my mind began to clear. Though I began to feel and think again coherently I still could not see. Two V.A.D.s fainted while help-ing with my dressings, the first during the day and the other at night. The second time I could not sleep and was calling out for someone to stop the beetles running down my face, when I heard my nurse say fiercely, "Get outside quick : don't make a fool of yourself here !" and the sound of footsteps moving towards the door. I remember cursing the unfortunate girl and telling her to put her head between her knees. I was told later that for my first three weeks I did little but curse and blaspheme, but I remember nothing of it. The nurses were wonderfully patient and never complained. Then one day I found that I could see. My nurse was bending over me doing my dressings, and she seemed to me very beautiful. She was. I watched her for a long time, grateful that my first glimpse of the world should be of anything so perfect. Finally I said :

"Sue, you never told me that your eyes were so blue."

For a moment she stared at me. Then, "Oh, Dick, how wonderful," she said. "I told you it wouldn't be long" ; and she dashed out to bring in all the nurses on the block.

I felt absurdly elated and studied their faces eagerly, gradually connecting them with the voices that I knew.

"This is Anne," said Sue. "She is your special V.A.D. and helps me with all your dressings. She was the only one of us you'd allow near you for about a week. You said you liked her voice." Before me stood an attractive fair-haired girl of about twenty-three. She smiled and her teeth were as enchanting as her voice. I began to feel that hospital had its compensations. The nurses called me Dick and I knew them all by their Christian names. Quite how irregular this was I did not discover until I moved to another hospital where I was considerably less ill and not so outrageously spoiled. At first my dressings had to be changed every two hours in the day-time. As this took over an hour to do, it meant that Sue and Anne had practically no time off. But they seemed not to care. It was largely due to them that both my hands were not amputated.

Sue, who had been nursing since seventeen, had been allocated as my special nurse because of her previous experience of burns, and because, as Matron said, " She's our best girl and very human." Anne had been married to a naval officer killed in the *Courageous*, and had taken up nursing after his death.

At this time there was a very definite prejudice among the regular nurses against V.A.D.s. They were regarded as painted society girls, attracted to nursing by the prospect of sitting on the officers' beds and holding their hands. The V.A.D.s were rapidly disabused of this idea, and, if they were lucky, were finally graduated from washing bed-pans to polishing bed-tables. I never heard that any of them grumbled, and they gradually won a reluctant recognition. This prejudice was considerably less noticeable in the Masonic than in most hospitals : Sue, certainly, looked on Anne as a companionable and very useful lieutenant to whom she could safely entrust my dressings and general upkeep in her absence. I think I was a little in love with both of them.

The Masonic is perhaps the best hospital in England, though at the time I was unaware how lucky I was. When war broke out the Masons handed over a part of it to the services ; but owing to its vulnerable position very few action casualties were kept there long. Pilots were pretty quickly moved out to the main Air Force Hospital, which I was not in the least eager to visit. Thanks to the kind-hearted duplicity of my house surgeon, I never had to ; for every time they rang up and asked for me he would say that I was too ill to be moved. The Masonic's great charm lay in that it in no way resembled a hospital ; if anything it was like the inside of a ship. The nursing staff were very carefully chosen, and during the regular blitzing of the district, which took place every night, they were magnificent.

The Germans were presumably attempting to hit Hammersmith Bridge, but their efforts were somewhat erratic and we were treated night after night to an orchestra of the scream and crump of falling bombs. They always seemed to choose a moment when my eyes were being irrigated, when my poor nurse was poised above me with a glass undine in her hand. At night we were moved into the corridor, away from the outside wall, but such was the snoring of my fellow sufferers that I persuaded Bertha to allow me back in my own room after Matron had made her rounds.

Bertha was my night nurse. I never discovered her real name, but to me she was Bertha from the instant that I saw her. She was large and gaunt with an Eton crop and a heart of gold. She was engaged to a merchant seaman who was on his way to Australia. She made it quite clear that she had no intention of letting me get round her as I did the day staff, and ended by spoiling me even more. At night when I couldn't sleep we would hold long and heated arguments on the subject of sex. She expressed horror at my ideas on love and on her preference for a cup of tea. I gave her a present of four pounds of it when I was discharged. One night the Germans were particularly persistent, and I had the unpleasant sensation of hearing a stick of bombs gradually approaching the hospital, the first some way off, the next closer, and the third shaking the building. Bertha threw herself across my bed ; but the fourth bomb never fell. She got up quickly, looking embarrassed, and arranged her cap.

" Nice fool I'd look if you got hit in your own room when you're supposed to be out in the corridor," she said, and stumped out of the room.

An R.A.S.C. officer who had been admitted to the hospital with the painful but unromantic complaint of piles protested at the amount of favouritism shown to me merely because I was in the R.A.F. A patriotic captain who was in the same ward turned on him and said: "At least he was shot down defending his country and didn't come in here with a pimple on his bottom. The Government will buy him a new Spitfire, but I'm damned if it will buy you a new arse."

One day my doctor came in and said that I could get up. Soon after I was able to totter about the passages and could be given a proper bath. I was still unable to use my hands and everything had to be done for me. One evening during a blitz, my nurse, having led me along to the lavatory, placed a prodigiously long cigarette-holder in my mouth and lighted the cigarette in the end of it. Then she went off to get some coffee. I was puffing away contentedly when the lighted cigarette fell into my pyjama trousers and started smouldering. There was little danger that I would go up in flames, but I thought it advisable to draw attention to the fact that all was not well. I therefore shouted "Oi!" Nobody heard me. "Help!" I shouted somewhat louder. Still nothing happened, so I delivered myself of my imitation of Tarzan's elephant call of which I was quite proud. It happened that in the ward opposite there was an old gentleman who had been operated on for a hernia.

The combination of the scream of falling bombs and my animal cries could mean only one thing. Someone had been seriously injured, and he made haste to dive over the side of the bed. In doing so he caused himself considerable discomfort : convinced of the ruin of his operation and the imminence of his death, he added his cries to mine. His fears finally calmed, he could see nothing humorous in the matter and insisted on being moved to another ward. From then on I was literally never left alone for a minute.

For the first few weeks, only my parents were allowed to visit me and they came every day. My mother would sit and read to me by the hour. Quite how much she suffered I could only guess, for she gave no sign. One remark of hers I shall never forget. She said : " You should be glad this has to happen to you. Too many people told you how attractive you were and you believed them. You were well on the way to becoming something of a cad. Now you'll find out who your real friends are." I did.

When I was allowed to see people, one of my first visitors was Michael Cary (who had been at Trinity with me and had a First in Greats). He was then private secretary to the Chief of Air Staff. He was allowed to stay only a short time before being shoo'd away by my nurses, but I think it may have been time enough to shake him. A short while afterwards he joined the Navy as an A.B. I hope it was not as a result of seeing me, for he had too good a brain to waste polishing brass. Colin came down whenever he had leave from Hornchurch and brought me news of the Squadron.

Ken MacDonald, Don's brother who had been with " A " Flight at Dyce, had been killed. He had been seen about to bale out of his blazing machine at 1000 feet ; but as he was over a thickly populated area he had climbed in again and crashed the machine in the Thames.

Pip Cardell had been killed. Returning from a chase over the Channel with Dexter, one of the new members of the Squadron, he appeared to be in trouble just before reaching the English coast. He jumped ; but his parachute failed to open and he came down in the sea. Dexter flew low and saw him move. He was still alive, so Dexter flew right along the shore and out to sea, waggling his wings to draw attention and calling up the base on the R.T. No boat put out from the shore, and Dexter made a crash landing on the beach, drawing up ten yards from a nest of buried mines. But when they got up to Pip he was dead.

Howes had been killed, even as he had said. His Squadron had been moved from Hornchurch to a quieter area, a few days after I was shot down. But he had been transferred to our Squadron, still deeply worried because as yet he had failed to bring anything down. The inevitable happened ; and from his second flight with us he failed to return.

Rusty was missing, but a clairvoyant had written to Uncle George swearing that he was neither dead nor captured. Rusty, he said (whom he had never seen), had crashed in France, badly burned, and was being looked after by a French peasant.

As a counter to this depressing news Colin told me that Brian, Raspberry, and Sheep all had the D.F.C., and Brian was shortly to get a bar to his. The Squadron's confirmed score was nearing the hundred mark. We had also had the pleasure of dealing with the Italians. They had come over before breakfast, and together with 41 Squadron we were looking for them. Suddenly Uncle George called out :

" Wops ahead."

" Where are they ? " asked 41 Squadron.

" Shan't tell you," came back the answer. " We're only outnumbered three to one."

Colin told me that it was the most unsporting thing he had ever had to do, rather like shooting sitting birds, as he so typically put it. We got down eight of them without loss to ourselves and much to the annoyance of 41 Squadron.

Then one day I had an unexpected visitor. Matron opened the door and said " Someone to see you," and Denise walked in. I knew at once who she was. It was unnecessary for her to speak. Her slight figure was in mourning and she wore no make-up. She was the most beautiful person I have ever seen.

Much has been written on Beauty. Poets have excelled themselves in similes for a woman's eyes, mouth, hair ; novelists have devoted pages to a geometrically accurate description of their heroines' features. I can write no such description of Denise. I did not see her like that. For me she had an inner beauty, a serenity which no listing of features can convey. She had a perfection of carriage and a grace of movement that were strikingly reminiscent of Peter Pease, and when she spoke it might have been Peter speaking.

" I hope you'll excuse me coming to see you like this," she said ; " but I was going to be married to Peter. He often spoke of you and wanted so much to see you. So I hope you won't mind me coming instead."

There was so much I wanted to say, so many things for us to talk over, but the room seemed of a sudden unbearably full of hurrying jolly nurses who would not go away. The bustle and excitement did little to put her at her ease, and her shyness was painful to me. Time came for her to leave, and I had said nothing I wanted to say. As soon as she was gone I dictated a note, begging her to come again and to give me a little warning. She did. From then until I was able to get out, her visits did more to help my recovery than all the expert nursing and medical attention. For she was the very spirit of courage. It was useless for me to say to her any of the usual words of comfort for the loss of a fiancé, and I did not try. She and Peter were two halves of the same person. They even wrote alike. I could only pray that time would cure that awful numbness and bring her back to the fullness of life. Not that she was broken. She seemed somehow to have gathered his strength, to feel him always near her, and was determined to go on to the end in the cause for which he had given his life, hoping that she too might be allowed to die, but feeling guilty at the selfishness of the thought.

She believed passionately in freedom, in freedom from fear and oppression and tyranny, not only for herself but for the whole world.

"For the whole world." Did I believe that? I still wasn't sure. There was a time — only the other day — when it hadn't mattered to me if it was true or not that a man could want freedom for others than himself. She made me feel that this might be no mere catch-phrase of politicians, since it was something to which the two finest people I had ever known had willingly dedicated themselves. I was impressed. I saw there a spirit far purer than mine. But was it for me? I didn't know. I just didn't know.

I lay in that hospital and watched summer turn to

winter. Through my window I watched the leaves of my solitary tree gradually turn brown, and then, shaken by an ever-freshening wind, fall one by one. I watched the sun change from a great ball of fire to a watery glimmer, watched the rain beating on the glass and the small broken clouds drifting a few hundred feet above, and in that time I had ample opportunity for thinking.

I thought of the men I had known, of the men who were living and the men who were dead; and I came to this conclusion. It was to the Carburys and the Berrys of this war that Britain must look, to the tough practical men who had come up the hard way, who were not fighting this war for any philosophical principles or economic ideals; who, unlike the average Oxford undergraduate, were not flying for aesthetic reasons, but because of an instinctive knowledge that this was the job for which they were most suited. These were the men who had blasted and would continue to blast the Luftwaffe out of the sky while their more intellectual comrades would, alas, in the main be killed. They might answer, if asked why they fought, " To smash Hitler ! " But instinctively, inarticulately, they too were fighting for the things that Peter had died to preserve.

Was there perhaps a new race of Englishmen arising out of this war, a race of men bred by the war, a harmonious synthesis of the governing class and the great rest of England; that synthesis of disparate backgrounds and upbringings to be seen at its most obvious best in R.A.F. Squadrons? While they were now possessed of no other thought than to win the war, yet having won it, would they this time refuse to step aside and remain indifferent to the peacetime fate of the country, once again leave government to the old governing class? I thought it possible. Indeed, the process might be said to have already begun. They now had as their representative Churchill, a man of initiative, determination, and no Party. But they would not always have him; and what then? Would they see to it that there arose from their fusion representatives, not of the old gang, deciding at Lady Cufuffle's that Henry should have the Foreign Office and George the Ministry of Food, nor figureheads for an angry but ineffectual Labour Party, but true representatives of the new England that should emerge from this struggle? And if they did, what then? Could they unite on a policy of humanity and sense to arrive at the settlement of problems which six thousand years of civilization had failed to solve? And even though they should fail, was there an obligation for the more thinking of them to try, to contribute at whatever personal cost " their little drop," however small, to the betterment of mankind? Was there that obligation, was that the goal towards which all those should strive who were left, strengthened and confirmed by those who had died? Or was it still possible for men to lead the egocentric life, to work out their own salvation without concern for the rest; could they simply look to themselves — or, more important, could I? I still thought so.

The day came when I was allowed out of the hospital for a few hours. Sue got me dressed, and with a pair of dark glasses, cotton-wool under my eyes, and my right arm in a sling, I looked fairly presentable. I walked out through the swing-doors and took a deep breath.

London in the morning was still the best place in the world. The smell of wet streets, of sawdust in the butchers' shops, of tar melted on the blocks, was exhilarating. Peter had been right: I loved the capital. The wind on the heath might call for a time, but the facile glitter of the city was the stronger. Self-esteem, I suppose, is one cause; for in the city, work of man, one is somebody, feet on the pavement, suit on the body, anybody's equal and nobody's fool; but in the country, work of God, one is nothing, less than the earth, the birds, and the trees; one is discordant — a blot.

I walked slowly through Ravenscourt Park and looked into many faces. Life was good, but if I hoped to find some reflection of my feeling I was disappointed. One or two looked at me with pity, and for a moment I was angry; but when I gazed again at their faces, closed in as on some dread secret, their owners hurrying along, unseeing, unfeeling, eager to get to their jobs, unaware of the life within them, I was sorry for them. I felt a desire to stop and shake them and say : " You fools, it's you who should be pitied and not I ; for this day I am alive while you are dead."

And yet there were some who pleased me, some in whom all youth had not died. I passed one girl, and gazing into her face became aware of her as a woman : her lips were soft, her breasts firm, her legs long and graceful. It was many a month since any woman had stirred me, and I was pleased. I smiled at her and she smiled at me. I did not speak to her for fear of breaking the spell, but walked back to lunch on air. After this I was allowed out every day, and usually managed to stay out until nine o'clock, when I drove back through the blitz and the black-out.

" London can take it " was already becoming a truism ; but I had been put out of action before the real fury of the night attacks had been let loose, and I had seen nothing of the damage. In the hospital, from the newspapers, and from people who came to see me, I gained a somewhat hazy idea of what was going on. On the one hand I saw London as a city hysterically gay, a city doomed, with nerves so strained that a life of synthetic gaiety alone prevented them from snapping. My other picture was of a London

bloody but unbowed, of a people grimly determined
to see this thing through, with man-power mobilized ;
a city unable, through a combined lack of inclination,
facility, and time, to fritter away the war in the night-
haunts of the capital. I set out to see for myself.

London night-life did exist. Though the sirens
might scream and the bombs fall, restaurants and cocktail bars remained open and full every night of the
week. I say restaurants and cocktail bars, for the
bottle parties and strip-tease cabarets which had a
mushroom growth at the beginning of the war had
long been closed. Nor was prostitution abroad.
Ladies of leisure whose business hours were from
eleven till three were perhaps the only citizens to find
themselves completely baffled by the black-out.
London was not promiscuous : the diners-out in a
West End restaurant were no longer the clientele of
café society, for café society no longer existed in
London. The majority of the so-called smart set felt
at last with the outbreak of war a real vocation, felt
finally a chance to realize themselves and to orientate
themselves to a life of reality. They might be seen in
a smart restaurant ; but they were there in another
guise — as soldiers, sailors, and airmen on forty-eight
hours' leave ; as members of one of the women's
services seeking a few hours' relaxation before again
applying themselves wholeheartedly to their jobs ; or
as Civil servants and Government workers who, after

a hard day's work, preferred to relax and enjoy the bombing in congenial company rather than return to a solitary dinner in their own flats.

While the bombs were dropping on London (and they were dropping every night in my time in the hospital), and while half London was enjoying itself, the other half was not asleep. It was striving to make London as normal a city by night as it had become by day. Anti-aircraft crews, studded around fields, parks, and streets, were momentarily silhouetted against the sky by the sudden flash of their guns. The Auxiliary Fire Service, spread out in a network of squads through the capital, was standing by, ready at a moment's notice to deal with the inevitable fires ; air-raid wardens, tireless in their care of shelters and work of rescue, patrolled their areas watchfully. One heavy night I poked my nose out of the Dorchester, which was rocking gently, to find a cab calmly coasting down Park Lane. I hailed it and was driven back to the hospital. The driver turned to me : " Thank God, sir," he said, " Jerry's wasting 'is time trying to break our morale, when 'e might be doing real damage on some small town."

With the break of day London shook herself and went back to work. Women with husbands in Government jobs were no longer to be seen at noon draped along the bars of the West End as their first appointment of the day. They were up and at work with determined efficiency in administrative posts of the Red Cross, the women's voluntary services, and the prisoners of war organizations. The Home Guards and air-raid wardens of the previous night would return home, take a bath, and go off to their respective offices. The soldier was back with his regiment, the airman with his squadron ; the charming frivolous creatures with whom they had dined were themselves in uniform, effective in their jobs of driving, typing, or nursing.

That, I discovered, was a little of what London was doing. But what was London feeling ? Perhaps a not irrelevant example was an experience of Sheep Gilroy's when flying with the Squadron. He was sitting in his bath when a " flap " was announced. Pulling on a few clothes and not bothering to put on his tunic, he dashed out to his plane and took off. A few minutes later he was hit by an incendiary bullet and the machine caught fire. He baled out, quite badly burned, and landed by a parachute in one of the poorer districts of London. With no identifying tunic, he was at once set upon by two hundred silent and coldly angry women, armed with knives and rolling-pins. For him no doubt it was a harrowing experience, until he finally established his nationality by producing all the most lurid words in his vocabulary ; but as an omen for the day when the cream of Hitler's Aryan youth should attempt to land in

Britain it was most interesting.

All this went on at a time when night after night the East End was taking a terrible beating, and it was rumoured that the people were ominously quiet. Could their morale be cracking? The answer was provided in a story that was going the rounds. A young man went down to see a chaplain whom he knew in the East End. He noticed not only that the damage was considerable but that the people were saying practically nothing at all. "How are they taking it?" he asked nervously. The chaplain shook his head. "I'm afraid," he said, "that my people have fallen from grace: they are beginning to feel a little bitter towards the Germans."

The understatement in that remark was impressive because it was typical. The war was practically never discussed except as a joke. The casual observer might easily have drawn one of two conclusions: either that London was spent of all feeling, or that it was a city waiting like a blind man, unseeing, uncaring, for the end. Either conclusion would have been wide of the mark. Londoners are slow to anger. They had shown for long enough that they could take it; now they were waiting on the time when it would be their turn to dish it out, when their cold rage would need more than a Panzer division to stamp it out.

Now and then I lunched at home with my mother, who was working all day in the Prisoners of War

Organization, or my father would leave his desk long enough to give me lunch at his club. On one of these occasions we ran into Bill Aitken, and I had coffee with him afterwards. He was still in Army Co-operation and reminded me of our conversation at Old Sarum. "Do you remember," he asked, "telling me that I should have to eat my words about Nigel Bicknell and Frank Waldron? Well, you were certainly right about Nigel."

"I haven't heard anything," I said, "but you sound as though he had renounced his career as Air Force Psychologist."

Bill laughed. "He's done more than that. He was flying his Blenheim to make some attack on France when one engine cut. He carried on, bombed his objective, and was on his way back when the other engine cut out too, and his machine came down in the sea. For six hours, until dawn when a boat saw them, he held his observer up. He's got the D.F.C."

"I must write to him," I said. "But I was right about Frank too. Do you remember your quotation that war was 'a period of great boredom, interspersed with moments of great excitement'; and how you said that the real test came in the periods of boredom, since anyone can rise to a crisis?"

"Yes, I remember."

"Well, I think I'm right in saying that Frank has come through on that score. He's in the Scots Guards with very little to do ; but he's considerably more subdued than you'll remember him. When he first got out of the Air Force he thought he could waltz straight into the Guards, but they wouldn't take him until he had been through an O.C.T.U. That was his first surprise. The second was when there was no vacancy in the O.C.T.U. for three months. Our Frank, undismayed, hied himself off to France and kicked up his heels in Megève with the Chasseurs Alpins, and then in Cannes with the local lovelies. But he came back and went through his course. He was a year behind all his friends — or rather all those that were left, and it sobered him up. I think you'd be surprised if you saw him now."

Bill got up to leave. " I should like to see him again," he said with a smile, " but of the ex-bad boys, I think you are the best example of a change for the better."

" Perhaps it's as well that you can't stay," I said. " I'm afraid it wouldn't take you long to see that you're mistaken. If anything, I believe even more strongly in the ideas which I held before. Sometime we'll discuss it."

I spent most evenings with Denise at the house in Eaton Place. It was the usual London house, tall, narrow, and comfortable. Denise was living there alone with a housekeeper, for her father was about to marry again and had moved to the country. At

tea-time I would come and find her curled up on the
sofa behind the tray, gazing into the fire ; and from
then until eight o'clock, when I had to drive back to
the Masonic, we would sit and talk — mostly of Peter,
for it eased her to speak of him, but also of the war,
of life, and death, and many lesser things.

Two years before the war she had joined the
A.T.S. Sensibility and shyness might well have made
her unsuited for this service, but when her family said
as much, they merely fortified her in her determination. After she was commissioned, she fainted on her
first parade, but she was not deterred, and she succeeded. She had left the A.T.S. to marry Peter. I
was not surprised to learn that she had published a
novel, nor that she refused to tell me under what
pseudonym, in spite of all my accusations of inverted
snobbery. She wished to see nobody but Colin and
me, Peter's friends ; and though often she would have
preferred to be alone, she welcomed me every day
nevertheless. So warm and sincere was her nature,
that I might almost have thought myself her only
interest. Try as I would, I could not make her think
of herself ; it was as if she considered that as a person
she was dead. Minutes would go by while she sat
lost in reverie, her chin cupped in her hand. There
seemed nothing I could do to rouse her to consciousness of herself, thaw out that terrible numbness, breathe
life into that beautiful ghost. Concern with self was

gone out of her. I tried pity, I tried understanding, and finally I tried brutality.

It was one evening before dinner, and Denise was leaning against the mantelpiece, one black heel resting on the fender.

"When are you coming out of mourning?" I asked.

She had been standing with her chin lowered; and now, without lifting it, she raised her eyes and looked at me a moment.

"I don't know," she said slowly. "Maybe I never shall."

I think she sensed that the seemingly innocent question had been put deliberately, though she couldn't yet see why. It had surprised her; it had hurt her, as I had meant it to. Up to now I had been at pains to tread delicately. Now the time had come, I felt, for a direct attack upon her sensibility under the guise of outward stupidity.

"Oh, come, Denise," I said. "That's not like you. You know life better than that. You know there's no creeping away to hide in a dream world. When something really tragic happens — the cutting-off of a man at a moment when he has most reason to live, when he has planned great things for himself — the result for those who love him isn't a whimpering pathos; it's growth, not decline. It makes you a richer person, not a poorer one; better fitted to

tackle life, not less fitted for it. I loved Peter too.
But I'm not going to pretend I feel sorry for you ;
and you ought to be grateful to the gods for having
enriched you. Instead, you mope."

I knew well enough that she wouldn't go under,
that this present numb resignation was transitory.
But I had been worried too long by her numbness,
her rejection of life, and I wanted to end it. She
said nothing, and I dared not look at her. I could
see her fingers move as I went doggedly on.

"You can't run away from life," I said. "You're
a living vital person. Your heart tells you that Peter
will be with you always, but your senses know that
absence blots people out. Your senses are the bound-
aries of your feeling world, and their power stops
with death. To go back and back to places where
you were happy with Peter, to touch his clothes, dress
in black for him, say his name, is pure self-deception.
You drug your senses in a world of dreams, but reality
cannot be shut out for long."

Still she said nothing, and I had a quick look at
her. This was far worse than badgering Peter in the
train. Her face was tense, slightly flushed, and her
eyes were wide-open and staring with what I hoped
was anger, not pain. I wished to rouse her, and prayed
only that I would not reduce her to tears.

"Death is love's crucifixion," I said brutally.
"Now you go out with Colin and me because we

were his friends, we are a link. But we are not only his friends, we are men. When I leave you, and say good-night, it's not Peter's hand that takes yours, it's mine. It's Colin's touch you feel when he helps you on with your coat. Colin will go away. I shall go back to hospital. What are you going to do then? Live alone? You'll try, but you won't be able. You will go out again — and with people who didn't know Peter, people your senses will force you to accept as flesh and blood, and not fellow players in a tragedy."

She went over to a sofa opposite me and sat looking out of the window. I could see her breast rise and fall with her breathing. Her face was still tense. The set of her head on her shoulders was so graceful, the lines of her figure were so delicate as she sat outlined against the light, that I became aware with a shock of never before having thought of her as a woman, a creature of flesh and blood. I who had made the senses the crux of my argument had never thought of her except as disembodied spirit. Minutes passed; she said no word; and her silence began almost to frighten me. If she should go on saying nothing, and I had to do all the talking, I didn't know quite what I should end by saying. I was about to attack her again when she spoke, but in a voice so gentle that at first I had trouble hearing her.

" You're wrong, Richard," she said. " You are so afraid of anything mystical, anything you can't analyse, that you always begin rationalizing instinctively, in self-defence, fearing your own blind spots. You like to think of yourself as a man who sees things too clearly, too realistically, to be able to have any respect for the emotions. Perhaps you don't feel sorry for me ; but I do feel sorry for you.

" I *know* that everything is not over for Peter and me. I know it with all the faith that you are so contemptuous of. We *shall* be together again. We are together now. I feel him constantly close to me ; and that is my answer to your cheap talk about the senses. Peter lives within me. He neither comes nor goes, he is ever-present. Even while he was alive there was never quite the tenderness and closeness between us that now is there."

She looked straight at me and there was a kind of triumph in her face. Her voice was now so strong that I felt there was no defeating her any more, no drawing her out of that morass of mysticism from which I so instinctively recoiled.

" I suppose you're trying to hurt me to give me strength, Richard," she said ; " but you're only hurting yourself. I have the strength. And let me explain where it comes from, so that we need never revert to the subject again. I believe that in this life we live as in a room with the blinds down and the lights on. Once or twice, perhaps, it is granted us to switch off the lights and raise the blinds. Then for a moment the darkness outside becomes brightness, and we have a glimpse of what lies beyond this life. I believe not only in life after death, but in life before death. This life is to me an intermission lived in spiritual darkness. In this life we are in a state not of being, but of becoming.

"Peter and I are eternally bound up together; our destinies are the same. And you, with your un-awakened heart, are in some curious way bound up with us. Oh, yes you are ! In spite of all your intellectual subterfuges and attempts to hide behind the cry of self-realization ! You lay in hospital and saw Peter die as clearly as if you had been with him. You told me so yourself. Ever since Peter's death you have been different. It has worked on you; and it's only because it has that I tell you these things. Colin says he would never have believed that anyone could change as you have."

"That," said I, "was pure hallucination. I don't pretend to account for it exactly, but it was that hundredth example of instinct, or intuition, that people are always boasting of while they never mention the ninety-nine other premonitions that were pure fantasy."

"Please, Richard," she said, "let's not talk about Peter and me any more. Your self-realization theory is too glib to stand a real test. To pass coldly through the death and destruction of war, to stand aloof and watch your sensibility absorb experience like a photographic plate, so that you may store it away to use for your own self-development — that's what you had hoped to do, I believe ? "

" Of course it is," I admitted. She was really roused now, and I was pleased.

" Well, you can't ! You know you can't, despite that Machiavellian pose of yours. You tell me women are not as I am. I tell you, men are not as you are. Or rather, were. You remember those photographs taken of you before the crash that I saw the other day ? Well, I believe that then, before the crash, you could and possibly did feel as you say you still do. I could never have liked you when you looked like that, looked like the man of the theory you still vaunt. Have you read Donne's *Devotions* ? "

" Looked through them," I said.

" In one of them he says this : ' Any man's death diminishes me, because I am involved in Mankind.' You too are involved, Richard ; and so deeply that you won't always be able to cover up and protect yourself from the feelings prompted in you by that involvement. You talk about my self-deception : do you really believe you can go through life to the end, always taking and never giving ? And do you really imagine that you haven't given to me, haven't helped me ? Well, you have. And what have you got out of it ? Nothing ! You have given to me in a way that would have been impossible for you before Peter's death. You are still giving. You are conferring value on life by feeling Peter's death as deeply as you do. And you are bound to feel the death, be recreated by the death, of the others in the Squadron — if not in the same degree, certainly in the same way. Certainly you are going to 'realize' yourself; but it won't be by leading the egocentric life. The effect that you will have on everybody you meet will come not only from your own personality, but from what has been added to you by all the others who are now dead — what you have so ungratefully absorbed from them."

She spoke with great feeling and much of what she said struck home. It was true that Peter was much in my thoughts, that I felt him somewhere near me, that he was in fact the touchstone of my sensibility at the moment. It was true that the mystical experience of his death was something which was outside my understanding, which had still to be assimilated, and yet, and yet . . . I could not help but feel that with the passage of time this sense of closeness, of affinity, must fade, that its very intensity was in part false, occasioned by being ill, and by meeting Denise so shortly afterwards; a Denise who was no mere shadow of Peter, but Peter's reincarnation; thus serving to keep the memory and the experience always before my eyes. While here were two people of an intense lyrical sensibility, two people so close in thought, feeling, and ideals, that although one was dead and the other living they were to me as one, yet I could not feel that their experience was mine, that it could do more than touch me in passing, for that I had been of any help to Denise was in a large part due to the fact that we were so dissimilar. While her thoughts came trailing clouds of glory, mine were of the earth earthy, and at such a time could help to strike a balance between the mystical flights of her mind and the material fact of high-explosive bombs landing in the next street. But though we might travel the same road for a time, lone voyagers eager for company, yet the time must come when our ways should part. Right or wrong, her way was not mine and I should be mistaken in attempting to make it so. We must live how we can.

# 7

## *The Beauty Shop*

I HAD now been in hospital something over two
months and it was thought that I was sufficiently
recovered for operation.

Shortly after my arrival at the Masonic the Air
Force plastic surgeon, A. H. McIndoe, had come up
to see me, but as I had been blind at the time I could
recollect his visit but vaguely, remembering only that
he had ordered the gentian violet to be removed from
my eyes and saline compresses to be applied instead,
with the result that shortly afterwards I had been able
to see.

He was expected this time at about eleven o'clock,
but I was ready a good hour before, bathed and shaved
and dressings elaborately correct. The charge nurse
ushered him in fussily. Of medium height, he was
thick-set and the line of his jaw was square. Behind
his horn-rimmed spectacles a pair of tired friendly
eyes regarded me speculatively.

" Well," he said, " you certainly made a thorough
job of it, didn't you ? "

He started to undo the dressings on my hands and

I noticed his fingers — blunt, capable, incisive. By
now all the tannic had been removed from my face
and hands. He took a scalpel and tapped lightly on
something white showing through the red granulating
knuckle of my right forefinger.

"Bone," he remarked laconically.

He looked at the badly contracted eyelids and the
rapidly forming keloids, and pursed his lips.

"Four new eyelids, I'm afraid, but you're not
ready for them yet. I want all this skin to soften up
a lot first. How would you like to go to the south
coast for a bit?"

He mentioned the official R.A.F. convalescent hospital on the south coast, generously supplied with golf
courses, tennis and squash courts. But as I could not
use my hands, and abhorred seaside resorts in winter,
I wasn't very enthusiastic. I asked instead whether I
could go down to a convalescent home a couple of
miles from his hospital. He raised no objection and
said that he would fix it with the Commandant.

"And I'll be able to keep an eye on you there,"
he added. He had got up to go when I asked him
how long it would be before I should fly again. I
had asked the same question on his previous visit, and
when he had said "Six months" I had been desperately depressed for days. Now when he said, "Next
war for you : those hands are going to be something
of a problem," I wasn't even surprised. I suppose

I had known it for some time. I felt no emotion at all.

He took his leave and I went off to have lunch with my mother.

Two days later, after the disentangling of a few cross wires in official circles, Air Ministry permission came through and I was driven down to Sussex.

The house was rambling and attractive, and ideal for a convalescent home. I was greeted at the door by Matron and led in to tea. There were about twenty other inmates drinking tea, mostly Army men, not particularly exciting and with not particularly exciting complaints. About them hung the listless air and furtive manner of undertakers, born no doubt of their prolonged inactivity combined with the dreary nature of their intestinal afflictions. By dinner-time I was preparing to resign myself to a comfortable if not stimulating period of relaxation, when a couple of genial souls came rolling in very late and I met Colin Hodgkinson and Tony Tollemache.

Hodgkinson was twenty and in the Fleet Air Arm : it was not until he got up after dinner that I noticed his two artificial legs. While training in an Albacore he had come into collision with a Hurricane. His two companions and the Hurricane pilot were killed instantly and Colin was found in a field six hours later.

Tony Tollemache had crashed in March, night flying. Coming in to land, his Blenheim had turned over and caught fire, throwing him free. His passenger was also thrown free and killed; but under the impression that he was still inside, Tony had climbed in again and wandered up and down the flaming machine, looking for him. He had been badly burned on his face, hands, and, above all, legs. For this action he got the Empire Gallantry Medal and nearly a year in hospital. He had already had several operations, and he was due at the hospital in another two days for a graft on his left hand.

We sat long by the glow of the open fire talking of many things and it was late when we finally climbed the stairs to bed. As I turned on my side and closed my eyes I was content. Tomorrow I should have my breakfast in bed, be given a bath, and come down only for lunch: I was the autocrat of the bolster, the aristocrat of fine linen: there were many worse ways of spending the war.

The following afternoon an eye specialist took a look at me: the pupil of my left eye, dilated by regular treatment with belladonna, interested him particularly.

"Can't close your eyes at all, can you?" he asked.

"No, sir," I said.

"Well, we'll have to get some covering over that left eye or you'll never use it again."

He went into the Commandant's office where there was a telephone, and returned a few minutes later.

" McIndoe is going to give you a new pair of top lids," he said. " I know your eyes are still infected but we'll have to take that chance. You're to go in with Tollemache tomorrow."

At the Masonic I had been the only action casualty. I had been very ill and in a private ward ; subsequently I had been outrageously spoiled. Having little previous experience of hospitals, I had taken it all as a matter of course. At the convalescent home the food was exceptional and the living conditions bordering on the luxurious : as a result the new hospital was something of a shock. It was one of several hundred Emergency Medical Service hospitals. Taken over by the Ministry of Health at the beginning of the war, these were nearly all small country-town hospitals in safe areas. Erected by subscription for the welfare of the district and run by committees of local publicity-loving figures in the community, they had been perfectly adequate for that purpose. They were not, however, geared for a war-time emergency ; they were too small. To overcome this difficulty the Ministry of Health had supplied them with " blisters " to accommodate the anticipated flow of troops. I had heard of these " blisters " and was vaguely aware that they were huts, but this hospital provided my first introduction to them.

It was of fairly recent construction and of only one story. There were two main wards : one re-

served for women and filled with residents of the
district ; the other for men, one half for local civilians
and the other (eight beds) for action casualties. Then
there were the " blisters " ; a dental hut, and two
others set at an angle to the main building.

Ward Three, housing some of the worst cases,
stood about fifty yards away from the hospital. It
was a long, low hut, with a door at one end and
twenty beds down each side. The beds were separated
from each other only by lockers, and it was possible
without much exertion to reach out and touch the
man in the next bed. Towards the far end the lockers
degenerated into soap-boxes. They constituted the
patients' furniture. Windows were let into the walls
at regular intervals on each side : they were never
open. Down the middle there was a table with a
wireless on it, a stove, and a piano. On either side
of the entrance passage were four lavatories and two
bathrooms. Immediately on the left of the entrance
passage was the saline bath, a complicated arrangement
of pipes that maintained a constant flow of saline
around the bathed patient at a regulated temperature.
McIndoe had been using it with great success for the
rapid healing of extensive burns. Next to this, in a
curtained-off bed, was a little girl of fifteen, by name
Joan, terribly burnt by boiling sugar her first day in
a factory. Joan was in this ward because there was
no other saline bath in the hospital (there were only

three in England), and she could not be moved any distance. She screamed fairly regularly, and always before being lifted into the bath ; her voice was thin and like that of a child of seven. As the time for her bath approached there was a certain tension throughout the hut ; and then everyone would start talking rather loudly, and the wireless was turned up.

For the rest, there was a blind man at the far end learning Braille with the assistance of his wife, a Squadron Leader, several pilot officers, a Czech, and sundry troops, unlikely to forget Dunkirk as quickly as most.

But my first taste of Ward Three was not yet. It was to the main building that I went for my new eyelids, and with little graciousness. Tony and I came in late, a fair measure of whisky inside us, and started noisily to get undressed. Our beds were next to each other : opposite us were two Hurricane pilots, one with his legs badly burned and the other with a six-weeks growth of beard and a thick surgical bandage over his eyes. He was being fed by a nurse.

" Is he blind ? " I whispered to Tony.

" Blind ? " he roared. " Not half as blind as we are, I'll bet. No, me boy. That's what you're going to look like tomorrow when McIndoe's through with you."

" Are you daft, Mr. Tollemache, coming in here late and making all that noise ? If it's trouble you want you'll get it when Sister Hall sees you. And tell your fine friend to take his shoes off the bed."

This was my first introduction to the Ward Charge Nurse. She rose from feeding the man with the bandaged eyes and stood feet apart and hands on hips, her cap awry, one tooth nibbling her lower lip as though it was lettuce.

Tony turned to me.

"Begad," he said, "I forgot to warn you, it's back in Hell's Kitchen we are. The ward is lousy with Irish and 'tis better to lie and rot than let them lay a finger on your dressings. They'll give you a dig for De Valera as soon as look at you."

"Ach! you needn't show off now, Mr. Tollemache. That's not funny and I'm not laughing."

She drew herself up to her full five feet and stalked majestically from the ward, somewhat spoiling the effect by a shrill cackle of laughter when she caught sight of the pair of red pyjamas that I was unpacking.

"It's the wrong address you're at with those passion pants," she said. "This is a hospital, not an English country house week-end."

"Be off with you, woman," I said, and putting on the offending garments I climbed into bed and settled down to read.

Shortly afterwards Sister Hall came into the ward, her dark-blue uniform proclaiming her rank.

"More Ireland," whispered Tony as she approached.

She stopped at the foot of my bed and I noticed that she was short, that her hair was grey, and that a permanent struggle between a tight-lipped mouth and smiling eyes was at the moment being very definitely won by the mouth.

"Good evening, Mr. Tollemache," she said.

"Good evening, Sister Hall," said Tony in his blandest manner.

She turned to me.

"Mr. Hillary, both you and Mr. Tollemache are to be operated on tomorrow morning. As you know, you should have been in earlier for preparation ; now it will have to be done in the morning. I hope you will settle in here quickly ; but I want it understood that in my ward I will tolerate no bad language and no rudeness to the nurses."

"My dear Sister," I replied, "I've no doubt that you will find me the mildest and most soft-spoken of men," and sitting up in bed I bowed gravely from the waist. She gave me a hard look and walked through the ward.

Tony waited until she was out of earshot. Then : "A tough nut, but the best nurse in the hospital," he said. "I don't advise you to get on the wrong side of her."

Shortly before the lights were put out McIndoe made a round of the ward followed by half a dozen assistants, mostly service doctors who were training

under him. " You're first on the list, Tony," he said,
" and you're second. By the looks of you both we'll
need to use a stomach pump before we can give you
any anaesthetic."

He took a look at my eyes. " They're still pretty
mucky," he said, " but I think you'll find it a relief
to have some eyelids on them." He passed on
through the ward and we settled down to sleep.

In the morning we were wakened early and
" prepped " by Taffy, the Welsh orderly. " Prep-
ping " consists of sterilizing the area of skin to be
used for the graft and shaving completely any sur-
rounding hair. My eyelids were to be a " Thiersch "
graft (a layer of skin thin as cigarette paper) taken
from the inside of my left arm, so Taffy shaved the
arm and armpit, then sterilized the arm and bound it
up in a loose bandage. He did the same thing to
Tony's leg, from where the skin was to be taken for
his hand, and we were both ready to go. The Charge
Nurse then trundled in a stretcher on wheels, parked
it beside Tony's bed, pushed his feet into an enormous
pair of bed socks, and whipped out a hypodermic
needle. This contained an injection to make one
drowsy half an hour before being wheeled into the
operating theatre.

" Bet you she's blunted the needle," said Tony ;
" and look at her hand ; it's shaking like an aspen
leaf."

" Be quiet, Mr. Tollemache, let's have less of your sauce now."

After much protesting she finally caught his arm and stuck him with the needle. He then climbed on to the trolley, which was screened off, and after about half an hour he was wheeled away.

I hoped that the operation would not be a lengthy affair, for I was hungry and could have no food until after I had been sliced up. Finally Tony was wheeled back, very white on the unburned patches of his face and breathing ether all over the room. It was my turn for the trolley. The injection did not make me particularly drowsy, and feeling bored I asked for a cigarette from one of the others and puffed away contentedly behind the screen. But I had not counted on the sharp eyes of Sister Hall. For a second she stared unbelievingly at the thin spiral of smoke ; then she was inside the screen, the confiscated cigarette glowing accusingly in her hand and herself looking down on me with silent disapproval. I gazed back innocently ; but pulling the screen to with a jerk, she walked on, her measured tread the silent voice of outraged authority.

It was time for me to go. Two nurses appeared at either end of the trolley and I was off, Tony's stertorous breathing and the coarse cries of the others following me down the ward. I was welcomed by the anaesthetist, vast and genial, with his apparatus that resembled a petrol station on wheels. As he was tying up my arm with a piece of rubber tubing, McIndoe came in sharpening his knife and wearing a skull-cap and multi-coloured gown, for all the world like some Bedouin chieftain. The anaesthetist took my arm and pushed the needle in gently. " Well, good-bye," he said. A green film rose swiftly up my throat and I lost consciousness.

When I came round I was not uncomfortable, and unlike Tony I was not sick. I could not see ; but apart from a slight pricking of the eyes I had no pain, and but for the boring prospect of five days without reading I was content. Those of us with eyelid grafts had of course to be fed and given bed baths, but we could (thank God) get up and walk to the lavatory, escorted by a nurse. Were there no nurses about, the others would sing out instructions to the needy one until he arrived safely at his destination.

Being unable to see, had, I discovered, some distinct disadvantages. As I could not read, I talked ; and as everyone knows, there are few more pleasant pastimes when one is indisposed than grousing and swearing. After a few unfortunate incidents I always asked Tony if any nurses were about before opening my mouth, but Tony was unreliable, getting a hideous pleasure out of watching the consequences. Then — I think it was on the third day of my incarceration — some nurse further down the ward dropped a bed-pan with a crash that made me start up in bed.

"Jesus Christ," I said, "what a hospital ! It stinks like a sewer, it's about as quiet as a zoo, and instead of nurses we've got a bunch of moronic Irish amazons."

"Mister Hillary !" The voice was so close that I almost fell out of bed.

"That's done it," I thought ; and I was right.

"Not another dressing do you get until you apologize." Sister Hall was standing at my elbow. Tony, of course, was delighted and I could hear him chuckling into the bed-clothes. I opened my mouth to apologize but no words came. Instead, I realized with horror that I was laughing, laughing in a manner that could in no way be passed off as a mere nervous titter, that could be taken, indeed, for nothing but what it was — a rich fruity belly-laugh.

Nothing was said, but I had a sense of impending doom. A few minutes later my suspicions were con- firmed : I felt my bed begin to move.

"What goes on ?" I asked.

"Two orderlies are shipping you off next door," said Tony. "They're going to separate us."

Now I had no wish to be separated from Tony. He was amusing to talk to, and especially at a time when I could not see, I felt the need of his presence. Further, there is nothing more depressing than being moved in hospital just after getting the feel of a ward. So I got out of bed. The orderlies were for a moment nonplussed; but, as Tony explained to them, their orders were to move the bed, not me. I could almost see their faces clear and I heard the bed being pushed through the door.

"Trouble ahead," said Tony. "Haven't enjoyed myself so much for ages."

Sure enough, a few minutes later Sister Hall returned accompanied by one of the younger surgeons, unhappy and embarrassed by the whole thing.

"Now what's all this?" he asked nervously.

"Well, among other things," I said, "I have told Sister Hall that I object to being treated as though I were still in a kindergarten."

"He said more than that, Doctor," said Sister Hall with some truth. "He and Mr. Tollemache together make it impossible to run the ward."

By this time the pettiness of it was boring me, and when the harassed doctor said that he could not interfere with Sister Hall's running of the ward I made no demur and allowed myself to be led off to the all-glass covered-in balcony extension of the ward to which my bed had been moved. I made some remark to Tony as I passed his bed but Sister had the last word.

"And we'll have no bad language while I'm in charge here," she said, and shut the door firmly behind me.

I found myself next to an Army doctor with smashed insides, sustained running into a stationary lorry in the black-out. He had difficulty in getting his breath and roared and whistled all night. I began to regret the haste of my outburst.

The hospital visiting hours were from two till four in the afternoon, a change from the Masonic and an arbitrary rule which in my present state of mind I considered nothing short of monstrous. Denise, who was now back in the A.T.S. with an important job, could get off only at odd moments but wanted to come and see me. I asked the Matron if she might be allowed to come in the morning if she could get down from London, and the Matron very reasonably agreed. Denise duly arrived and called up from the station to ask when she might appear. Due to a mis-understanding, she was told that visiting hours were from two till four, and she had therefore to kick her heels for several hours in the town. By this time I was so enjoying my sense of persecution that, even if I had realized that it was a misunderstanding, I should doubtless have chosen to ignore the fact. When, therefore, on the stroke of four Sister Hall entered and said coldly, " All visitors must leave now," I would willingly have committed murder, but Denise laid a warning hand on mine and I held my peace.

The next day McIndoe took down the dressing from my eyes and I saw again.

" A couple of real horse blinkers you've got there," he said ; and indeed for a day or so that is what they felt like. In order to see in front of me I had to turn my face up to the ceiling. They moulded in very rapidly, and soon I could raise and lower them at will. It was a remarkable piece of surgery, and an operation in which McIndoe had yet to score a failure.

Shortly afterwards I was allowed to have a bath and soak the bandage off my arm from where the graft had been taken. This laborious and painful process had already taken me half an hour when Sister Hall came in. I was down to the last layer, which I was pulling at gingerly, hurting myself considerably in the process.

"Well, really, Mister Hillary!" she said; and taking hold of it she gave a quick pull and ripped the whole thing off cleanly and painlessly.

"Christ!" I started involuntarily, but stopped myself and glanced apprehensively at Sister's face. She was smiling. Yes, there was no doubt about it, she was smiling. We said nothing, but from that moment we understood each other.

Tony's graft had been a success, and within a few days we were allowed out for a fortnight's convalescence before coming in again for further operations.

As I was getting ready to go, Sister took me on one side and slipped a small package into my hand.

"You'll be wanting to look your best for the girls, Mr. Hillary, and I've put in some brown make-up powder that should help you."

I started to protest but she cut me short.

"You'll be in again in a couple of weeks," she said. "Time enough for us to start quarrelling then."

We returned after a short but very pleasant convalescence — Tony for his last operation, one top lid, and I for two lower ones.

The time when the dressings were taken down I looked exactly like an orang-outang. McIndoe had pinched out two semicircular ledges of skin under my eyes to allow for contraction of the new lids. What was not absorbed was to be sliced off when I came in for my next operation, a new upper lip. The relief, however, was enormous, for now I could close my eyes almost completely and did not sleep with them rolled up and the whites showing like a frightened negro.

Once again we retired to our convalescent home, where our hostess did everything possible to relieve the monotony of our existence. She gave a large party on Christmas night, and every few weeks brought down stage or screen people to cheer up the patients.

There had been some changes among the other inmates since our last visit, and two of de Gaulle's Frenchmen had arrived from an Aldershot hospital. One of them, an Army officer, had been in plaster since Dunkirk, where he got an explosive bullet in the arm. The other had been in the French Air Force but had decidedly un-Gallic features. When I first saw him he was wearing a beard and looked like a Renaissance Christ. Later he shaved it off and was indistinguishable from any chorus-boy in the second row.

When France fell he was completing his flying training in Morocco. He had taken off in an anti-quated trainer and landed at Gibraltar. Eventually he managed to reach England and to continue his training on Magisters with French instructors whom he described as old, blind, and incompetent. Apparently he was sent up to practise spins without having been told how to come out of them. His command of English was picturesque and somewhat erratic, yet he managed to convey to me a vivid picture of his crash.

" I am diving at about 4000 feet," he said, " when I start the spin. I am told only two turns, so after these I think I centralize the stick and rudder and come out. Nothing happens, so I cross the controls, open the gas and push the stick further forward. I do not wish to jump out, you understand, as I have done this before and do not like. So I try an inverted loop but nothing happens. By this time I have done many turns and am feeling dizzy, so I say to myself, ' I must now bale out,' and I undo my straps and stand up. When I look over the side a haystack is

# The Beauty Shop

spinning round the plane and I am stepping over the side, when crash ! And we are no more."

A most remarkable recital ! His back and one foot were broken. His body and leg were swathed in plaster of Paris, and his fellow-countryman, who was an artist, had painted the picture of the crash across his chest.

On Tuesdays and Thursdays the inmates always drove into town in the station wagon to go to the pictures. This involved sitting in the local tea-shop for an hour afterwards, eating sickening cakes and waiting for the car to drive them back. As tea-shops have the most appalling effect on me, depression descending like a fog, I seldom went along. Eliot has said the final word about them :

> Over buttered scones and crumpets
> Weeping, weeping multitudes
> Droop in a hundred A B C's.

But on our first Thursday out of the hospital our two Frenchmen asked Tony and me to accompany them, and we duly set off.

We were having tea when a pretty waitress came up and said to my bearded friend, "*Vous êtes Français ?*"

" *Oui, et vous ?* "

" *Canadienne-Française.* "

" *Dommage que je n'aille mieux. J'aimerais vous prouver que je vous trouve gentille.* "

211

" *Faudrait aussi que je le veuille !* "

" *N'importe. J'aimerais toujours tenter la chance.* "

The rest of us sat there like cold suet.

Tony and I went often to London, where we settled ourselves down in some restaurant, ordered a most excellent dinner, and surveyed the youth and beauty around us with a fatherly eye. For while we were now medically fit and perfectly content, yet we were still naturally enough drained of any exuberance of youthful vitality.

One night over a particularly good dinner I summed it up to Tony. " Well," I said, waving a vague hand at the crowded dance floor, " we're a lucky pair. Here we are enjoying all the pleasures of old men of sixty. To us it has been granted to pass through all the ages of man in a moment of time, and now we know the joys of the twilight of man's existence. We have come upon that great truth, that the warmth in the belly brought on by brandy and cigars leaves a glow that is the supreme carnal pleasure. Not for us the exacerbation of youthful flesh-twitchings, not for us palpitations and agony of spirit at a pretty smile, a slender waist. We see these things with pleasure, but we see them after our own fashion — as beauty, yes, and as a joy for ever, but as beauty should be seen, from afar and with reverence and with no desire to touch. We are free of the lusts of youth. We can see a patch of virgin snow and we do not have to rush out and leave our footprint. We are as David in the Bible when ' they brought unto him a virgin but he gat no heat.' "

Tony nodded owlishly and lit a cigar. Then, jabbing it through the air to emphasize his words, he spoke. Slowly and deliberately and with great sorrow he spoke.

" Alas," he said, " it is but a dream, a beautiful, beautiful dream, but still a dream. Youth will catch us up again. Youth with all her temptations, trials, and worries. There is no escape." He lowered his voice and glanced nervously over his shoulder. " Why, even now I feel her wings fluttering behind me. I am nearly the man I was. For you there is still a little time, not much but a little. Let us then enjoy ourselves while yet we may. Waiter, more brandy ! "

One night when we were in town we walked around to see Rosa Lewis at the Cavendish Hotel. Suddenly caught by a stroke, she had been rushed to the London Clinic, where she refused to allow any of the nurses to touch her. After a week she saw the bill and immediately got up and left.

When we arrived, there she was, seventy-six years old, shrieking with laughter and waving a glass of champagne, apparently none the worse. She grabbed me by the arm and peered into my face. " God, aren't you dead yet either, young Hillary ? Come here and I'll tell you something. Don't you ever die.

In the last two weeks I've been right up to the gates of 'eaven and 'ell and they're both bloody ! "

A few weeks later a heavy bomb landed right on the Cavendish, but Rosa emerged triumphant, pulling bits of glass out of her hair and trumpeting with rage. Whatever else may go in this war, we shall still have Rosa Lewis and the Albert Memorial at the end.

Thus did I while away the time between operations, living from day to day, sometimes a little bored, a little depressed, aware of being restless, but analysing this restlessness no further than as the inevitable result of months in bed.

# 8

## *The Last of the Long-Haired Boys*

IT was already January of 1941 when I returned to the hospital for the removal of the ledges under my eyes and the grafting of my new upper lip.

I had lunch at home, saying good-bye to London with two dozen oysters and a bottle of Pol Roget, and just caught my train. On the way down I began to regret the richness of my lunch and I was in no way cheered by the discovery that the only available bed was in Ward Three. McIndoe came round on his tour of the ward, and I asked if I might be first on the list, feeling that the great man would be at his best in the early morning. It was true that he never seemed to tire. Indeed he had been known to operate all day, and finally at ten o'clock at night, stretch himself comfortably and say to an exhausted theatre staff, " Now let's *do* something ! "

I was wakened early to have my arm " prepped " by one of the orderlies. I had decided on the arm, and not the leg, in order to be spared the bother of shaving my new upper lip. We chose a piece of skin bounded on one side by a vaccination mark and on the other by the faint scar of what are now my upper lids.

Sister gave me an injection at about nine o'clock, and an hour later, wearing my red pyjamas for luck, I climbed on to the trolley and was wheeled across the fifty yards of open space to the hospital. There was something a little lowering about this journey on a cold morning, but I reached the theatre feeling quite emotionless, rather like a business man arriving at his office. The anaesthetist gave me an injection and I lost consciousness.

On coming round, I realized that I was bandaged from forehead to lip and unable to breathe through my nose. At about three o'clock Tony Tollemache and his mother came to see me; I had by then developed a delicate froth on both lips and must have resembled a perhaps refined stallion. They were very kind, and talked to me quite normally. I'm afraid I replied little, as I needed my mouth to breathe with. They went at about four. After that the day was a blur : a thin wailing scream, the radio playing " Each day is one day nearer," injections, a little singing, much laughter, and a voice saying, " Naow, Charlie, *you* can't do it ; naow, Charlie, you *can't* do it ; naow, Charlie, you can't *do* it." After this, oblivion, thank God.

The next morning I awoke in a cold sweat after a nightmare in which my eyelids were sewn together and I was leading the Squadron in an Avro Tutor. In the evening one of the doctors took the bandages off my eyes. I was left with a thick dressing across my upper lip which pressed against my nose, and two sets of semicircular stitches under my eyes. Peering into a mirror, I noticed that my right eyebrow had been lifted up higher to pair it off with the left. This was also stitched. Later McIndoe made a round and peered anxiously at the scar under my right eye, which was blue and swollen. He moved on. There was comparatively little noise, but the ward smelt and I was depressed.

The next few days remain in my memory as a rather unpleasant dream. Rumour started that eight of us were to be isolated, owing to suspicion of a bug. It proved true. We climbed on to trolleys and were pushed across the yard to one of the main wards, from which a bunch of protesting old women had been evacuated. On the way over I passed a new victim of tannic acid being wheeled in to take my bed : all I could see was an ebony-coloured face enveloped in a white cowl. As we were pushed up the steps to our new quarters we were greeted by four nurses wearing masks, white aprons, and rubber gloves. Our luggage followed, and was tipped into the store-room outside.

Opposite me was Squadron Leader Gleave with a flap graft on his nose and an exposed nerve on his forehead : in Ward Three he had been unable to sleep, nor could the night nurse drug him enough to stop the pain. Next to him was Eric Lock, a tough little Shropshireman who had been with me at Hornchurch and collected twenty-three planes, a D.S.O., a D.F.C. and a bar : he had cannon-shell wounds in the arms and legs. On my left was Mark Mounsdon who trained with me in Scotland and was awaiting an operation on his eyelids. Beyond the partition was Joseph, the Czech sergeant pilot, also with a nose graft ; Yorkey Law, a bombardier, blown up twice and burned at Dunkirk, with a complete new face taken in bacon strips from his legs, and no hands ; and Neft, a clever young Jew (disliked for it by the others), with a broken leg from a motor-cycle accident.

We were of course allowed no visitors and could write no letters.

On the second day Neft's face began to suppurate and a small colony of streptococci settled comfortably on the Squadron Leader's nose. The rest of us waited grimly. Neft showed a tendency to complain, which caused Eric Lock to point out that some of us had been fighting the war with real bullets and would be infinitely grateful for his silence.

On the third day in our new quarters the smell of the bandage under my nose became so powerful that I took to dosing it liberally with eau-de-cologne.

I have since been unable to repress a feeling of nausea whenever at a party or in company I have caught a whiff of this scent.

Our heads were shorn and our scalps rubbed with special soap and anointed with M & B powder. We submitted to this with a varying amount of protestation : the Squadron Leader was too ill to complain, but Eric Lock was vociferous and the rest of us sullen. A somewhat grim sense of humour helped us to pass this day, punctuated by half-hours during which Neft was an object of rather cruel mockery. He had been a pork butcher before the war and of quite moderate means, but he made the mistake of mentioning this fact and adding that foul-mouthed talk amused him not at all. From that moment Yorkey Law, our bombardier, gave him no peace and plied him with anecdotes which even curled what was left of my hair. By the evening Neft had retired completely under the bed-clothes, taking his suppurating face with him.

After the huts our new ward was luxurious : the beds were more comfortable, and above each a pair of ear-phones hung on the wall. A large plain window ran the whole length of one side and ensured an adequate ventilation : the ward was kept dusted and tidy.

The nurses were efficient and not unfriendly, though the enforced wearing of masks and rubber gloves made them a little impersonal. Our language was always rough and sometimes offensive ; Eric, with an amiable grin on his face, would curse them roundly from dawn till dusk, but they seldom complained. They did their best to make up to us for our lack of visitors. Tony Tollemache came down once from the convalescent home and said good-bye through the window : he was returning to Hornchurch. Otherwise we saw nobody.

It was announced that our swabs had returned. We all clamoured to know who was, and who was not, infected. Apparently two were not, but which two the doctors would not say.

On February 14 I developed earache. Short of breath and completely blocked in the nose, I gave a snort and felt something crack in my right ear. Never having had earache before, I found the experience disagreeable to a degree : it was as though someone with a sharp needle was driving it at regular intervals into the side of my head.

An ear, nose, and throat man, on a course of plastic surgery under McIndoe, came along to see me. He regarded me dispassionately for a minute, and then withdrew with Sister to the other end of the ward. That night I was put on to Prontosil and knew beyond any doubt that I had the streptococcus.

I slept fitfully, aided in my wakefulness by the pain in my ear, Eric's snores, and the groans of the Squadron Leader.

In the morning the pain in my ear was considerable and I felt sick from the Prontosil. But it was now eight days since my operation, and the dressing on my lip was due to be taken down. For this mercy I was grateful, as the smell under my nose was proving too strong for even the most frequent doses of eau-de-cologne. At lunch-time one of the doctors took off the bandages and removed the stitches, at the same time cutting the stitches from under my eyes to the accompaniment of appreciative purrs from his satellites. I asked for a mirror and gazed at the result. It was a blow to my vanity : the new lip was dead white, and thinner than its predecessor.

In point of fact it was a surgical masterpiece, but I was not in the mood to appreciate it. I fear I was not very gracious. The lip was duly painted with mercurochrome, and the doctors departed. The relief at having the bandages removed was enormous, but I still dared not blow my nose for fear that I should blow the graft away. I took a bath and soaked the bandage off the arm from which my lip had been taken. This was a painful process lasting three-quarters of an hour, at the end of which time was revealed a deep narrow scar, neatly stitched. Sister then removed the stitches. During this little operation an unfortunate incident occurred. As soon as the stitches were out, instead of behaving in an approved and conventional manner and remaining pressed together, the two lips of the wound opened out like a fan, exposing a raw surface the size of a half orange. Everyone clustered round to inspect this interesting phenomenon but were hastily ordered back to bed by a somewhat harassed Sister.

That night I slept not at all : the pain in my ear was a continuous throbbing and I felt violently sick from the Prontosil. At about two o'clock I got up and started pacing the ward. A night nurse ordered me back to bed. I invited her to go to hell with considerable vigour, but I felt no better. She called me a wicked ungrateful boy and I fear that I called her a cow. Finally I returned to bed and attempted to read until morning.

In the conversation of the next twenty-four hours I took little part but lay, propped up in bed, watching the Squadron Leader rubbing his eye with pieces of cotton-wool. The hair from his scalp was making it acutely uncomfortable. This is not so odd as it sounds, for during a flap graft on the nose the scalp is brought down to the top of one's eyebrow where it is neatly rolled and feeds the new nose. It is of course shaved but the hair tends to grow again.

February 17 was a Friday, the day on which an ear, nose, and throat specialist was in the habit of visiting the hospital. It was arranged for me to see him, and putting on my dressing-gown, I walked along to the Out-patients' Department. His manner was reassuring. He felt behind my ear and inquired if it pained me. I replied that it did.

That being so he regretted the necessity, but he must operate within half an hour for what appeared to be a most unpleasant mastoid. I asked if I might be moved to Sister Hall's ward, and after one look at my face the doctors very decently agreed.

I went back, changed into my red pyjamas and climbed once more on to the trolley. I was wheeled along to the Horsebox, the title affectionately bestowed on the emergency theatre which was the converted end of the children's ward. McIndoe was already at work in the main theatre.

With the usual feeling of relief I felt the hypodermic needle pushed into my arm, and within five seconds I was unconscious.

For the next week I was very ill, though quite how seriously I could only judge by the alacrity with which all my requests were granted. I was again in the glass extension of Sister Hall's ward and she nursed me all day and most of the night. I had regular morphia injections and for long periods at a time I was delirious. The bug had got into my lip and was biting deep into the skin at three places. I remember being in worse pain than at any time since my crash. After the plastic operations I had felt no discomfort, but now with the continuous throbbing agony in my head I thought that I must soon go mad. I would listen with dread for the footsteps of the doctors, knowing that the time was come for my dressings, for the piercing of the hole behind my ear with a thin steel probe to keep it open for draining, a sensation that made me contract within myself at the mere touch of the probe on the skin.

It was during my second night in the glass extension that a 2500 lb. bomb landed a hundred yards away but did not explode. I heard it coming down with a curious whirring rustle, and as I heard it I prayed, prayed that it would be near and bring with it peace, that it would explode and take with it me, the extension, the ward, the huts, everything. For a moment I thought it had, so great was the force of impact, but as I realized slowly that it had not exploded I found that the tears were pouring down my face : I was sobbing with mingled pain, rage, and frustration. Sister immediately gave me another morphia injection.

It was decided that while the excavation squad was digging it out, everybody possible must be evacuated to the convalescent home. Those who were too ill to be moved would go to Ward Three on the far side of the hospital. I imagined that I would go along with the others, but after taking a look at me McIndoe decided that it would be too dangerous to move me. Sister Hall offered to send a special nurse with me, but they thought even so the risk was too great.

Sister looked at me : " I'm afraid that means the

huts," she said. At that something exploded inside me. McIndoe's chief assistant came into the ward to arrange for me to be moved and I let fly. I had not spoken since my operation and I saw the surprise in his face as I hauled myself up in bed and opened my mouth. Wild horses, I said, would not drag me back to that garbage-can of human refuse. If anyone laid a finger on my bed I would get up and start to walk to London. I preferred to die in the open rather than return to that stinking kitchen of fried flesh. I had come into the hospital with two scars on my upper lip : now I had a lip that was pox-ridden and an ear with enough infection in it to kill a regiment. There was only one thing to be said for the British medical profession : it started where the Luftwaffe left off. An outburst to which I now confess with shame, but which at the time relieved my feelings considerably.

" You're not making this very easy," he answered mildly.

" You're damn right, I'm not," I said, and then felt very sick and lay down.

It was then that Sister Hall was magnificent.

" I think perhaps he should stay here in his present state, sir," she said. " I'll see if I can fix up something."

The doctor, only too willing to have the problem off his hands, looked grateful, and left. I saw that she was smiling.

" Well, Mr. Hillary," she said, " quite like old

times," and went off to see what she could arrange. Somehow she obtained permission to convert one of the consulting rooms further down the hospital into a ward, and my bed was pushed along.

That night McIndoe came in to see me. He was still wearing his operating robes and sat down on the end of the bed. He talked to me for some time — of the difficulties of running a unit such as this, of the inevitable trials and set-backs which must somehow be met. He knew, he said, that I had had a tough break, but I must try not to let it get me down. I noticed that he looked tired, dead tired, and remembered that he had been operating all day. I felt a little ashamed. The next day my mother and Denise motored down to see me. I was grey in the face from all the Prontosil that I was taking and they both thought that I was on the way out, though of this they gave no sign. Poor Mother. The crash, the sea, the hospital, the operations — she had weathered them all magnificently. But this last shock was almost too much. She did not look very well.

During the last five months I had gradually built up to my usual weight of twelve stone, but in the next week I sweated my temperature down to normal and my weight down to nine stone. I also began to feel more human, and as the bomb had been removed and the evacuated ones brought back, I returned to the main ward and the regular hospital routine.

If there is one thing I really loathe it is to be awakened an hour earlier than necessary with a cup of cold brown tea. Unfortunately I could not approach Tony's imperious sarcasm, which was proof against all nurses until nine o'clock, but I finally hit on an idea for stopping this persecution. Nurse Courtney promised that if I made no more remarks about Ireland, she would no longer wake me with tea. I agreed with alacrity, saying that I could easily dispense with both. She at once bristled but was calmed down by Sister.

My God, I thought, who would be a nurse! They must suffer all the inconveniences of convent celibacy without the consolation of that inner glow which I take to be an integral part of the spiritual life.

It was shortly after this that Edmonds was re-admitted to the hospital and placed in the bed next to mine. He was the worst-burned pilot in the Air Force to live. Taking off for his first solo in a Hampden at night, he had swung a little at the end of his run and put a wing in. The machine had immediately turned over and burst into flames. He had been trapped inside and fried for several minutes before they dragged him out. When he had first been brought to McIndoe he had been unrecognizable and had lain for months in a bath of his own suppuration. McIndoe performed two emergency operations and then left it to time and careful dressings to heal him enough for more.

Never once had Edmonds complained. After nine months McIndoe had sent him away to build up his strength. Now he was back. It would take years to build him a new face. He was completely cheerful, and such was his charm that after two minutes one never noticed his disfigurement.

He was first on the list for operation the day after his readmission. Both his top lids and his lower lip were done together and he was brought back to the ward, even-tempered as ever. The man on his other side diverted him for most of the day with endless funny stories of crashes. Sometimes I think it would be very pleasant to be invested with the powers of life and death.

Three days went by and I noticed an ominous dribble down Edmonds' right cheek from under the dressing across his eyes. That night McIndoe took the dressing down : the right eyelid graft had not taken. He took it off and threw it away : it was the streptococcus at work again, and bitterly ironical that McIndoe's first eyelid failure should be on Edmonds. He was immediately put on to Prontosil and by the next morning was a greeny blue, with his lower lip jutting out like an African tribeswoman's.

After lunch some idiotic woman came in and exclaimed at how marvellously well he looked. I held my breath but I need not have worried. Instead of turning his face to the wall or damning her soul, he managed to smile and said :

" Yes, and I'm feeling much better too."

I could not but marvel at his self-control and un-ruffled good manners. I remembered a few of my own recent outbursts and felt rather small.

Here was a twenty-six-year-old South African with no ties in this country, no mere boy with his whole life to make, terribly injured without even the satis-faction of having been in action. Sometimes he be-haved as though he had been almost guilty not to have been shot down, as though he were in the hospital under false pretences ; but if ever a pilot deserved a medal it was he. He read little, was not musical, yet somehow he carried on. How ? What was it that gave not only him but all these men the courage to go on and fight their way back to life ? Was it in some way bound up with the consciousness of death ? This was a subject which fascinated me and I had discussed it with McIndoe. Did people know when they were about to die ? He maintained that they did not, having seen over two hundred go, none of them conscious that their last moment had come.

" How about Charles the Second's apology for being such an unconscionable time a-dying ? "

He admitted that in some cases people might have a premonition of death, but in cases of terrible physical injury he would say never. Their physical and mental conditions were not on a different plane : the first weakened the second (if I report him accurately), and there was neither consciousness of great pain nor realization of the finality of physical disintegration.

That, then, would account for my calmness when in the sea. I knew well enough, meanwhile, that sheer anger had pulled me through my mastoid complication. But what of the men who, after the first instinctive fight to live, after surviving the original physical shock, went on fighting to live, cheerfully aware that for them there was only a half-life ? The blind and the utterly maimed — what of them ? Their mental state could not remain in the same dazed condition after their bodies began to heal. Where did they get the courage to go on ?

It worried me all day. Finally I decided that the will to live must be entirely instinctive and in no way related to courage. This nicely resolved any suspicion that I might recently have behaved rather worse than any of the others, might have caused unnecessary trouble and confusion. Delighted with my analysis of the problem, I settled myself to sleep.

The following day my ear surgeon told me that I might go back to the convalescent home in a week, McIndoe told me that he would not operate on me again for three months, and my mother came down from town and told me that Noel Agazarian had been killed.

# The Last of the Long-Haired Boys

At first I did not believe it. Not Noel. It couldn't happen to him. Then I realized it must be true. That left only me — the last of the long-haired boys. I was horrified to find that I felt no emotion at all.

That left only me — the last of the long-haired

9

## *" I see they got you too "*

I WAS back at the convalescent home when the
letter came. I was very comfortable, but I had a
flat, let-down feeling. I suppose it was natural
enough after the mastoid ; but I knew it went deeper
than that. The last few months in the hospital had
most certainly been an experience. I had asked no
more than that of the war. I was by no means regretting it, but it was still too near in time for me to focus
it clearly. I had, I thought, observed the people
around me disinterestedly. Their suffering and pain
had in no way affected my attitude to the war. I had
come through it without falling a victim to the cloying
emotions of false pity. I could congratulate myself
that I was self-centred enough to have survived any
attack on my position as an egocentric. I had a fleeting
suspicion that that might be because the others had
been so much an integral part of my own experience
that I could consider them only in relation to myself ;
but I dismissed the idea. And yet something was
wrong.

My thoughts were no longer tuned to Peter :

there was no contact, not even through Denise. All this was now as nothing. I was back where I had started. It had been a mere passing emotional disturbance, occasioned by my weakened condition. With the passage of time, as I had foreseen, the whole relationship took on its normal proportions. Indeed I was a little irritated with Denise. What had seemed sensibility now seemed sentimentality: life was not all giving and selflessness, and no projection of the imagination could make it so. The realization that I had felt so deeply the need for the ghostly awareness of Peter now angered me. Still, I had not expected it to last. Why, then, this absurd feeling of futility ?

I was suddenly tired. The first intimation of spring was in the air and I went for walks in the garden. Crocuses were bursting out of the ground, the trembling livingness of the earth seemed urgent through the soles of one's shoes ; it was the time of poetry and the first glance of love ; yet I turned from it. It seemed to me that my mind was dry bone. I had an idea for a play to be called Dispersal Point, a study in Air Force mentality more or less on the lines of *Journey's End*, but the idea was stillborn. I was cold and emptied of feeling. It was as though I were again at school, at school and for Sunday lunch : the bars on the windows, the cracked plaster above the empty grate, the housemaster surreptitiously picking his teeth with a penknife, and the boys, their long-tailed coats drooping over the hardwood benches, crouched dispiritedly above sickening plates of cold trifle. And then one morning, the letter.

It was from David Rutter : he had read the notice about Noel in the paper and asked if I could come to see him. David Rutter, a man with, in a different way, as great an integrity as Peter's ; David and the awful sincerity of his pacificism, rationalized at Oxford by talk of the Middle Ages, field-boots under the surplice, a different war for the unemployed labourer and the Duke of Westminster ; but with an instinctive, deep-rooted hatred of killing which no argument could touch.

I had not seen him since that day more than a year before when Noel and I had got our commissions. We were in the bar of a London club, celebrating. David Rutter had come in. His first appeal as a conscientious objector had been turned down by the board that morning. We told him our news.

"You always were the lucky bastard, Richard," he said, and laughed. He had a drink with us and left. And now he was working on the land. I was eager to see if and how he had changed. I remembered our conversation at Oxford : I wasn't going to get hurt ; I should get killed or win some putty medals while he went to jail. Well, I had to admit it hadn't worked out quite like that.

The letter came as a relief. I was eager to go, was sure that something would come of the visit. I thought I might go to London for the night afterwards : it would be a change. I applied for two days' leave and caught a train to Norfolk.

David met me at the station. A lock of hair hung over his forehead and he wore an old tweed jacket and corduroy trousers : he looked very fit. He seemed glad to see me, and as we climbed into his small car he told me shyly that he was married. I said little while we drove. I was uncertain what approach to take and felt it safer to let him make the first move. He was uneasy and I felt guilty : I had such an unfair advantage. We drew up outside a square brick bungalow and got out.

" Well, here we are," said David with an attempt at a smile. " Come and meet Mary."

His wife greeted me politely but defensively. She was a large, good-looking girl, blond hair hanging loosely forward over her shoulders. She began at once to talk — about birds and their use as an alarm clock. She resented my face. I was amused and relieved, for the usual feminine opening of " Poor boy, how you must have suffered " embarrassed me ; embarrassed me not because it was tactless, but because I could not immediately disabuse my sympathizers of their misplaced pity without appearing mock-modest or slightly insane. And so I remained an impostor.

They would say, "I hope someone got the swine who got you : how you must hate those devils!" and I would say weakly, "Oh, I don't know," and leave it at that. I could not explain that I had not been injured in their war, that no thoughts of "our island fortress" or of "making the world safe for democracy" had bolstered me up when going into combat. I could not explain that what I had suffered I in no way regretted ; that I had welcomed it ; and that now that it was over I was in a sense grateful for it and certain that in time it would help me along the road of my own private development.

Well, here at least I need not worry.

Mary was still talking, this time about books, in an aggressive monologue which I was pretty certain masked a rawly sensitive nature.

But David cut in.

"It's all right, Mary," he said in a tired voice, "Richard's not belligerent." He turned to me apologetically : "I'm afraid I don't see many of my old friends any more and when I do there's usually a scene, so Mary's a bit on the defensive."

We talked for a while on safe subjects — his work on the land, the district, and his evening visits to the local pub to gossip with the villagers. David was restless, pacing continuously up and down the room and rubbing a nervous hand over his hair. His wife followed his every movement ; her eyes never left him. I realized that she was a very unhappy woman. It was not that she had no faith in David, for she was desperately loyal ; it was that he no longer had any faith in himself.

I wanted to start him off, so I asked him what the C.O. boards had been like.

" Oh, moronic but well-meaning," he said. " Yes, they were certainly moronic ; but they were right. That's the hell of it."

He sat down and stared moodily into the fire.

Then : " I'm sorry about Noel," he said.

" Yes," I said.

For a moment he sat in silence. Then he lay back in his chair and began to talk. From time to time he would glance up at my face, and as he talked I realized that while I might carry my scars for a few years, the scars of his action would be with him always. For he was a broken man. In the last year he had stood by and watched his ideals shattered, one by one. As country after country had fallen to Hitler his carefully reasoned arguments had been split wide open : it was as much the war of the unemployed labourer as of the Duke of Westminster. Never in the course of history had there been a struggle in which the issues were so clearly defined. Although our peculiar form of education would never allow him to admit it, he knew well enough that it had become a crusade. All this he could have borne. It was the painful death of his passionate fundamental belief that he should raise his hand against no man which finally brought his world crumbling about his ears.

It started as a suspicion, at first faint, then insistent, and finally a dominant conviction, that in this too, this in which he believed above all things, he had been wrong.

"After much heart-searching," he said, "I finally decided that with the outbreak of war I had failed in my own particular struggle. I had not now the right to refuse to fight : it was no longer a question for personal conscience but for the conscience of civilization. Civilization had decided, and it would be intolerable arrogance for me to question that decision."

He gave me a wry smile.

"It is to be regretted," he said, "that it has taken me more than a year to see this. Now I suppose I shall join up. Do you think I should ?"

I started : the question had caught me unawares. I looked at David's set face and the taut, expectant figure of his wife, and sitting there smugly with the "honourable" scars of a battle that was not mine I felt of a sudden very small.

"I don't know, David," I said. "That's a question which only you can decide."

When I rose to leave it was already dark. I said good-bye to his wife, and David drove me to my train up to London. As we got out of the car the searchlights were making a criss-cross pattern of light in the sky : all around us was the steady roar of anti-aircraft fire.

David held out his hand.

" Good-bye, Richard," he said. " You always were the lucky bastard."

And this time he meant it.

There was a heavy raid on and the train crawled interminably, only the dull-blue light in the ceiling and the occasional glow of a cigarette revealing the presence of the passengers. David by now would be home again, pacing the floor, up and down, up and down, while Mary sat by helpless. David, so lost and without purpose ; I had never expected to find him like that. I thought of Noel, of the two Peters, of the others in the Squadron, all dead ; and how the David that I had known was dead too. They had all, in their different ways, given so much : it was ironical that I who had given least should alone have survived.

Liverpool Street Station was a dull-grey blur of noise and movement. I managed somehow to get hold of a taxi and make a start across London, but my driver seemed doubtful whether we should be able to go very far. Some machine dropped a flare, and in the sudden brightness before it was put out I saw that the street was empty. What cars there were, were parked along the kerb and deserted.

" I'm afraid we'll be stopped soon, sir," said the

taxi-driver. At that moment there was a heavy crump unpleasantly close and glass flew across the street.

" See if you can find a pub and we'll stop there," I shouted.

A few yards further on he drew in to the kerb and we got out and ran to a door under a dimly lit sign of " The George and Dragon." Inside there was a welcoming glow of bright lights and beery breaths, and we soon had our faces deep in a couple of mugs of mild and bitter.

In one corner on a circular bench that ran round a stained wooden table sat a private in battle-dress and a girl, the girl drinking Scotch. She had light-brown hair and quite good features. I suppose if one had taken her outside and washed her face under a pump she would have had a rather mousy look, but she would still have been pretty. She was pretty now in spite of the efforts that she had made to improve on nature, had made and continued to make, for every few minutes she would take out a vanity case, pull a face into the mirror, lick her lower lip and dash her lipstick in a petulant streak of scarlet across her mouth. She was also talking very loud and laughing immoderately. I caught the barmaid's eye. She gave me a conspiratorial wink and shook her head knowingly ; ah yes, we understood, we two. But she was wrong : the girl was not drunk, she was very, very frightened, and, I thought, with good reason. For though at the Masonic I had dozed off regularly to the lullaby of the German night offensive, I had never before heard anything like this. The volume of noise shut out all thought, there was no lull, no second in which to breathe and follow carefully the note of an oncoming bomber. It was an orchestra of madmen playing in a cupboard. I thought, " God ! what a stupid waste if I were to die now." I wished with all my heart that I was down a shelter.

" We'd be better off underground tonight, sir, and no mistake." It was my taxi-driver speaking.

" Nonsense," I said. " We couldn't be drinking this down there," and I took a long pull at my beer.

I was pushing the glass across the counter for a refill when we heard it coming. The girl in the corner was still laughing and for the first time I heard her soldier speak. " Shut up ! " he said, and the laugh was cut off like the sound track in a movie. Then everyone was diving for the floor. The barmaid (she was of considerable bulk) sank from view with a desperate slowness behind the counter and I flung myself tight up against the other side, my taxi-driver beside me. He still had his glass in his hand and the beer shot across the floor, making a dark stain and setting the sawdust afloat. The soldier too had made for the bar counter and wedged the girl on his inside. One of her shoes had nearly come off. It was an inch from my nose : she had a ladder in her stocking.

My hands were tight-pressed over my ears but the detonation deafened me. The floor rose up and smashed against my face, the swing-door tore off its hinges and crashed over a table, glass splinters flew across the room, and behind the bar every bottle in the place seemed to be breaking. The lights went out, but there was no darkness. An orange glow from across the street shone through the wall and threw everything into a strong relief.

I scrambled unsteadily to my feet and was leaning over the bar to see what had happened to the unfortunate barmaid when a voice said, " Anyone hurt ? " and there was an A.F.S. man shining a torch. At that everyone began to move, but slowly and reluctantly as though coming out of a dream. The girl stood white and shaken in a corner, her arm about her companion, but she was unhurt and had stopped talking. Only the barmaid failed to get up.

" I think there is someone hurt behind the bar," I said. The fireman nodded and went out, to return almost immediately with two stretcher-bearers who made a cursory inspection and discovered that she had escaped with no more than a severe cut on the head. They got her on to the stretcher and disappeared.

Together with the man in the A.F.S., the taxi-driver and I found our way out into the street. He turned to us almost apologetically. " If you have nothing very urgent on hand," he said, " I wonder if you'd help here for a bit. You see it was the house next to you that was hit and there's someone buried in there."

I turned and looked on a heap of bricks and mortar, wooden beams and doors, and one framed picture, unbroken. It was the first time that I had seen a building newly blasted. Often had I left the flat in the morning and walked up Piccadilly, aware vaguely of the ominously tidy gap between two houses, but further my mind had not gone.

We dug, or rather we pushed, pulled, heaved, and strained, I somewhat ineffectually because of my hands ; I don't know for how long, but I suppose for a short enough while. And yet it seemed endless. From time to time I was aware of figures round me : an A.R.P. warden, his face expressionless under a steel helmet ; once a soldier swearing savagely in a quiet monotone; and the taxi-driver, his face pouring sweat.

And so we came to the woman. It was her feet that we saw first, and whereas before we had worked doggedly, now we worked with a sort of frenzy, like prospectors at the first glint of gold. She was not quite buried, and through the gap between two beams we could see that she was still alive. We got the child out first. It was passed back carefully and with an odd sort of reverence by the warden, but it was dead. She must have been holding it to her in the bed when the bomb came.

Finally we made a gap wide enough for the bed to be drawn out. The woman who lay there looked middle-aged. She lay on her back and her eyes were closed. Her face, through the dirt and streaked blood, was the face of a thousand working women; her body under the cotton nightdress was heavy. The nightdress was drawn up to her knees and one leg was twisted under her. There was no dignity about that figure.

Around me I heard voices. "Where's the ambulance?" "For Christ's sake don't move her!" "Let her have some air!"

I was at the head of the bed, and looking down into that tired, blood-streaked, work-worn face I had a sense of complete unreality. I took the brandy flask from my hip pocket and held it to her lips. Most of it ran down her chin but a little flowed between those clenched teeth. She opened her eyes and reached out her arms instinctively for the child. Then she started to weep. Quite soundlessly, and with no sobbing, the tears were running down her cheeks when she lifted her eyes to mine.

"Thank you, sir," she said, and took my hand in hers. And then, looking at me again, she said after a pause, "I see they got you too."

Very carefully I screwed the top on to the brandy flask, unscrewed it once and screwed it on again, for I had caught it on the wrong thread. I put the flask into my hip pocket and did up the button. I pulled

across the buckle on my great-coat and noticed that I
was dripping with sweat. I pulled the cap down over
my eyes and walked out into the street.

Someone caught me by the arm, I think it was the
soldier with the girl, and said : " You'd better take
some of that brandy yourself. You don't look too
good " ; but I shook him off. With difficulty I kept
my pace to a walk, forcing myself not to run. For I
wanted to run, to run anywhere away from that scene,
from myself, from the terror that was inside me, the
terror of something that was about to happen and
which I had not the power to stop.

It started small, small but insistent deep inside of
me, sharp as a needle, then welling up uncontrollable,
spurting, flowing over, choking me. I was drowning,
helpless in a rage that caught and twisted and hurled
me on, mouthing in a blind unthinking frenzy. I
heard myself cursing, the words pouring out, shrill,
meaningless, and as my mind cleared a little I knew
that it was the woman I cursed. Yes, the woman that
I reviled, hating her that she should die like that for
me to see, loathing that silly bloody twisted face that
had said those words : " I see they got you too."
That she should have spoken to me, why, oh Christ,
to me ? Could she not have died the next night, ten
minutes later, or in the next street ? Could she not
have died without speaking, without raising those cow
eyes to mine ?

" I see they got you too." All humanity had been in those few words, and I had cursed her. Slowly the frenzy died in me, the rage oozed out of me, leaving me cold, shivering, and bitterly ashamed. I had cursed her, cursed her, I realized as I grew calmer, for she had been the one thing that my rage surging uncontrollably had had to fasten on, the one thing to which my mind, overwhelmed by the sense of something so huge and beyond the range of thought, could cling. Her death was unjust, a crime, an outrage, a sin against mankind — weak inadequate words which even as they passed through my mind mocked me with their futility.

That that woman should so die was an enormity so great that it was terrifying in its implications, in its lifting of the veil on possibilities of thought so far beyond the grasp of the human mind. It was not just the German bombs, or the German Air Force, or even the German mentality, but a feeling of the very essence of anti-life that no words could convey. This was what I had been cursing — in part, for I had recognized in that moment what it was that Peter and the others had instantly recognized as evil and to be destroyed utterly. I saw now that it was not crime ; it was Evil itself — something of which until then I had not even sensed the existence. And it was in the end, at bottom, myself against which I had raged, myself I had cursed. With awful clarity I saw myself suddenly as I was. Great God, that I could have been so arrogant !

How long I had been walking I don't know, but the drone of aircraft had ceased, so the All Clear must have sounded. I had a horror of thinking, of allowing my mind to look back armed with this new consciousness, but memories of faces, scenes, conversations flooded in, each a shock greater than the last. I was again in the train with Peter, on the way to Edinburgh, sitting forward on the seat, ridiculing his beliefs with glib patronizing assurance. Once again I was drawing from him his hopes and fears, his aspirations for a better life, extracting them painfully one by one, and then triumphant, holding them up to the light, turning them this way and that, playing with them for a moment only to puncture them with ridicule and, delighted with my own wit, to throw them carelessly aside. Once again Peter was sitting opposite me, unruffled and tolerant, saying that I was not quite unfeeling, predicting that some shock of anger or of pity would serve to shake me from the complacency of my ivory tower, Peter quoting Tolstoi to me :

Man, man, you cannot live entirely without pity !

words which I had taken it upon myself to dismiss as the sentimental gub of an old man in his dotage.

Oh, God, that memory might be blotted out ; but it was remorseless. Peter's death lived by me in all its vivid intensity, offering me yet again the full life by all its implications, but rejected by me later to Denise. Rejected brutally, " Let the dead bury their dead," close the door on the past, be grateful for the experience, use it, but understand that there is no communication, no message, no spiritual guidance, no bridge between life and death. Go on, do not look back, there is nothing there, nothing ; it is all over. Denise, who had not been angry, who was now working day and night with Peter beside her, who had shown me the way, who with patience and understanding had let me look into her heart that I might learn. And I who, having looked, closed my eyes and turned away not wishing to believe, turned away irritated. Something there to be absorbed perhaps, an experience which might be useful ; very interesting emotionally of course, but nothing more. No, decidedly not. Dangerous morbid introspection ; must get away.

Noel, Peter Howes, Bubble, and the others — their deaths. Not felt quite as fully as one had expected perhaps, but then there was a war on, people dying every minute, one must harden one's heart. They were gone ; good friends all of them, but there it was, nothing there for me, no responsibility, no answering to them for my actions before or after.

And the hospital. I saw myself again that first day in Sussex, standing in the doorway and looking down

Ward Three. Once again I saw Joan in the bed by the saline bath, saw her hairless head, her thin emaciated face, and heard that voice like a child of seven's whimpering, saw myself register it vaguely and pass on to look with interest at the others. The blind man learning Braille, utterly dependent on his wife ; bad that, should be helping himself. Joseph the Czech and his nose growing from his forehead ; his hands messy stumps and his eyes stupidly trusting. The one with practically no face at all, just a pair of eyes ; unable to talk of course, but interesting, oh yes, particularly interesting : Yorkey Law the bombardier, later to be invalided out, but quite fascinating with all those bacon strips off his legs gradually forming a face. And the others ; one after another I remembered them until finally Edmonds — Edmonds and his year of pain and disfigurement and my nice comfortable little theory on his will to live.

I remembered them all, remembered how at first they had interested me in their different ways, and then how they had irritated me with their dumb acceptance of the hospital conditions, their gratitude for what was being done for them, and above all their silent, uncomplaining endurance. It had baffled me. I had felt their suffering a little, had seen it, but through a glass darkly. They were too close to me, too much a part of my own suffering for me to focus it like this thing tonight.

# The Last Enemy

Tonight. Had it really been such a short time ago, had it been today that I had talked to David Rutter?

Again memory dragged me back. It had been I this very day who had sat back smoking cigarettes while David had poured out his heart, while his wife had watched me, taut, hoping. But I had failed. I had been disturbed a little, yes, but when he was finished I had said nothing, given no sign, offered no assurance that he was now right. I saw it so clearly.

"Do you think I should join up?" On my answer had depended many things, his self-respect, his confidence for the future, his final good-bye to the past. And I had said nothing, shying away from the question, even then not seeing. In the train I had crossed my legs and sat back, amused, God help me, by the irony of it all. They had given so much and were dead. I had given so little and was alive. Ah, well!

I was very grateful for the night and my solitude. I who had always repeated the maxim "Know thyself" was seeing now what it meant to live by that maxim. "Le sentiment d'être tout et l'évidence de n'être rien." That was me. The feeling that I was everything and the evidence that I was nothing.

So Peter had been right. It was impossible to look only to oneself, to take from life and not to give except

250

by accident, deliberately to look at humanity and then
pass by on the other side. No longer could one say
" The world's my oyster and the hell with the rest."
What was it Denise had said ? " Yes, you can realize
yourself, but not by leading the egocentric life. By
feeling deeply the deaths of the others you are conferring value on life."

For a moment I had had it, had that feeling, but
I had let it go, had encouraged it to go, distrusting it,
and now, and now . . . was it, then, too late ?

I stopped and looked up into the night. They
were there somewhere, all of them around me ; dead
perhaps, but not gone. Through Peter they had
spoken to me, not once but often. I had heard and
shrugged my shoulders ; I had gone my way un-
heeding, not bitter, either on their account or mine,
but in some curious way suspended, blind, lifeless, as
they could never be.

Not so the others. Not so the Berrys, the Staple-
tons, the Carburys. Again instinct had served. They
hadn't had even the need of a Peter. They had felt
their universe, not rationalized it. Each time they
climbed into their machines and took off into combat,
they were paying instinctive tribute to their comrades
who were dead. Not so those men in hospital. They
too knew, knew that no price was too dear to achieve
this victory, knew that their discomforts, their suffering, were as nothing if they could but get back, and

should they never get back they knew that silence was their rôle.

But I ! What had I done ? What could I do now ?

I wanted to seize a gun and fire it, hit somebody, break a window, anything. I saw the months ahead of me, hospital, hospital, hospital, operation after operation, and I was in despair. Somehow I got myself home, undressed, and into bed and fell into a troubled sleep. But I did not rest ; when I awoke the problem was still within me. Surely there must be something.

Then after a while it came to me.

I could write. Later there would be other things, but now I could write. I had talked about it long enough, I was to be a writer, just like that. I was to be a writer, but in a vacuum. Well, here was my chance. To write I needed two things, a subject and a public. Now I knew well enough my subject. I would write of these men, of Peter and of the others. I would write for them and would write with them. They would be at my side. And to whom would I address this book, to whom would I be speaking when I spoke of these men ? And that, too, I knew. To Humanity, for Humanity must be the public of any book. Yes, that despised Humanity which I had so scorned and ridiculed to Peter.

If I could do this thing, could tell a little of the lives of these men, I would have justified, at least in some measure, my right to fellowship with my dead, and to the friendship of those with courage and steadfastness who were still living and who would go on fighting until the ideals for which their comrades had died were stamped for ever on the future of civilization.

THE END

PRINTED BY R. & R. CLARK, LTD., EDINBURGH